God's Hiddenness in Combat

Toward Christian Reflection on Battle

Preston Jones and Cody Beckman

University Press of America,® Inc.
Lanham · Boulder · New York · Toronto · Plymouth, UK

Copyright © 2009 by
University Press of America,® Inc.
4501 Forbes Boulevard
Suite 200
Lanham, Maryland 20706
UPA Acquisitions Department (301) 459-3366

Estover Road
Plymouth PL6 7PY
United Kingdom

Library of Congress Control Number: 2008943384
ISBN-13: 978-0-7618-4534-8 (paperback : alk. paper)
eISBN-13: 978-0-7618-4535-5

For Annemarie.
Asgwrn o'm hesgyrn, a chnawd o'm cnawd.

—P.J.

For Kara and my parents. Thank you for everything.

—C.B.

And for JBU friends
Ron Maines, Gary Riley, and Layden Stroud
who have been there.

Contents

Acknowledgements

I began interviewing combat veterans in my history classes in the late 1990s. I was teaching then at a public university, so I did not ask many theological questions. By 2000 I had moved to a Christian preparatory high school. I was surprised to find that when I did ask Christian war veterans questions about the place of faith in the world of combat, all but one had little or nothing to say. Most acknowledged that, during war, their spiritual lives had been put on hold. One, forgetting that I had been the interviewer, later told me about a previous researcher who had asked him many "irrelevant" questions about his time as a fighter pilot in the Pacific. One of the irrelevant questions was whether the pilot prayed before going out on combat missions.

Like many, I assumed the basic truthfulness of the famous statement "there are no atheists in foxholes." I assumed that, since death is so close to them, combatants would be driven to think about the meaning of life and about their relationship with the divine. I was surprised to find that the opposite was usually the case. I came to believe that the other famous quip about war—that it is "hell"—seemed more accurate. It was surprising to see that men, who otherwise were quite articulate about their Christian faith, had a difficult time placing God in the world of war in any definite and personal way. Those who did talk about God in the context of battle regularly referred to the God of the early books of the Old Testament, with some also pointing to grim passages in the New Testament book of Revelation. Aside from a few references to Jesus' chasing of the merchants out of the temple, the central figure of Christianity is much harder to place in the realm of combat. It was these observations that led me to begin work on this monograph.

I am grateful to the Faculty Development Committee at John Brown University for funding that made possible a research trip to the National Museum of the Pacific War in Fredericksburg, Texas, in the summer of 2006. The committee also made possible dozens of interviews with combat veterans. I am grateful to my colleagues at JBU who put me in touch with veterans. The Lee Balzer Lecture committee at JBU invited me to speak on the topic of this book to the faculty in August of 2006, and JBU made it financially possible for me to give a talk on God's hiddenness in combat a month later at the Conference on Faith and History meeting at Oklahoma Baptist University. I was later able to address some of the topics raised in these pages in talks given to the Rotary Club and American Legion Post in Siloam Springs, Arkansas. Members of all audiences asked good questions.

Of course, I want to thank the many veterans who took the time to speak to me in the years 1998-2007, in Santa Rosa, California; Dallas, Texas; Siloam Springs, Arkansas; and Eagle River, Alaska. Most of the interviews with veterans were public, and all the veterans knew that I was pursuing a research project.

But because I did not obtain permission to quote the veterans, this manuscript leaves them anonymous. However, I do wish particularly to thank Layden Stroud (WWII) and Ron Maines (Vietnam) for fielding my questions on several occasions over a space of years.

I thank Barry Hankins (Baylor University), Tim Stafford (*Christianity Today*), Henry Robertson (Louisiana College), Michael Hamilton (Seattle Pacific University), Graeme Hunter (University of Ottawa), Gregory Bloomquist (St. Paul's University), and Catherina Hurlburt (*Breakpoint Worldview*), as well as my JBU colleagues Gary Guinn and Trisha Posey, for their comments on and criticisms of an earlier version of this work. Students of mine—Ellen Gaston, Kelly Neighbors, Jonathan VerHoeven, Peter Helman, and Luke Hayes— brought useful sources to my attention.

Finally, I am indebted to Cody Beckman, a former student of mine and an excellent historian in the making. Neither Cody nor I have ever faced combat (though I did serve in the U.S. Navy), but we do share an interest in the experience and consequences of battle. Cody pointed me to many excellent sources and he conducted interviews of his own in New London, Iowa; Springdale, Arkansas; and via email. His senior thesis at JBU was on this manuscript's topic; he presented his research to faculty and students at JBU in the spring of 2007. Initially I planned to thank him in these acknowledgements for his great assistance. But as time went by, and as his contribution grew, it seemed better to consider him a co-laborer, for that is what he really is.

Preston Jones
Siloam Springs, Arkansas

Introduction

Christian reflection on warfare has typically taken the path either of pacifism or just war theory. The Christian intellectual community is grateful to the thinkers and scholars who, over the centuries, have pursued these lines of thought and documented Christian experience in the face of war.[1] Yet whether a war is just, or whether Christians should ever be directly involved in wars, is irrelevant to a nineteen year old Nebraskan who finds himself in a firefight in southern Afghanistan. Just war theory means nothing to a kid from Harlem now walking through a minefield. The finer points of pacifism cannot help a twenty-three year old helicopter pilot trying to extract wounded comrades while under enemy fire.

Yes, young men and women may volunteer for military service partly motivated by assumptions about the justice of a war.[2] It is true that, before and after combat, warriors may conclude, paradoxically, that war is sometimes necessary to bring about greater peace.[3] Fighters may be at ease within themselves, knowing that they are pursuing God's purpose for their lives.[4] They may even conclude that war is needed to make safe the preaching of the Gospel.[5] And it is true that, when warriors reflect on their time in battle, they can come to see it as providing spiritual analogies—such as one pilot who likened the spiraling down of a plane disabled by ground fire to the spiraling of a life lived outside the will of God.[6]

Conversely, the experience of war may push a former combatant toward pacifistic non-involvement, while, for theological reasons, other pacifists may volunteer to serve as non-combatant medics. For some, the suffering that war caus-

---

1. See, for example, James O. Lehman and Steven M. Nolt, *Mennonites, Amish, and the American Civil War* (Baltimore: Johns Hopkins University Press, 2007), xi.

2. Major General Barry McCaffrey said in the early 1990s that the U.S. Army at that time was "the most religious Army since the Army of Northern Virginia during the Civil War." The writers of this monograph have not seen substantial evidence to support this claim. Even if it is true, however, personal religious faith matters in a conscious way before and after battle, not during battle. McCaffrey is quoted, and his words are contextualized, in Stephen Mansfield, *The Faith of the American Soldier* (New York: Penguin, 2005), 33-5.

3. In *Beyond Tragedy: Essays on the Christian Interpretation of History* (New York: Charles Scribner's Sons, 1937), Reinhold Niebuhr quotes St. Augustine: "The peace of the world is based in strife" (180).

4. Chuck Holton, *A More Elite Soldier* (Sisters, OR: Multnomah Publishers, 2003), 19-20.

5. Clyde H. Denis, ed., *These Live On: The Best of True Stories Unveiling the Power and Presence of God in World War II* (Chicago: Good Books, 1945).

6. Geoff Gorsuch, *On Eagles Wings: The Spiritual Odyssey of a Young American Pilot in Vietnam* (Colorado Springs: NavPress, 1989), 134-5.

es leads to a loss of faith in a benevolent God, while others see that "[s]uffering is the location of the hidden God."[7]

Having fought, it is difficult for combat veterans not to philosophize in one way or another. If nothing else, battle puts one's own soul to the test.[8] But when the bullets fly—when the napalm cascades to earth—when the gate on the landing craft opens—philosophy goes out the door. Combat is about survival. In a battle zone there is no room for intellectual abstractions or soul-searching.[9] Between flights, one pilot in Vietnam came to see that God does not take sides in war but, as he prepared for another mission, he realized that reflection needed to be put on hold. "I'd now be operating on instinct," he writes. "The age-old instinct to survive."[10]

This slim volume has been written with the combatant in mind. It seeks to find an answer to the question, Where is God for the twenty-year-old Marine throwing a hand grenade? Or for the teenager who has just lost an arm or a face to an enemy's bomb? Where is Jesus for the exhausted medic or nurse? Where is God for the insurgent setting a booby trap? Where is Jesus for the kid engaged in hand-to-hand fighting on Peleliu, among the costliest battle zones of the Second World War? To face these questions is to see the inadequacy of just war and pacifist theory, at least in the context of battle.

Obviously, combat is about survival. But not everyone survives, and many of those who return from war still lose something on the battlefield—youthful innocence, limbs, peace of mind, simplistic ideas about God, and the possibility of warm relationships with others. So combat is also about suffering.

Christianity, too, is about suffering. This study aims to help combat veterans and those who care about them, along with readers interested in the effects war has on people, to see the experience of war in the heavy but powerful light of the crucifixion of Jesus.[11] It is no surprise that the one person who "got it" at

---

7. Claudia M. Nolte, "A Theology of the Cross for South Africa," *Dialog: A Journal of Theology* 42:1 (2003), 53.
8. Mansfield, *Faith of the American Soldier*, 9.
9. Bruce H. Norton, *Force Recon Diary, 1969* (New York: Ivy Books, 1991), 236. Also see Richard Schweitzer, *The Cross and the Trenches: Religious Faith and Doubt among British and American Great War Soldiers* (Westport, CT: Praeger, 2003),132-4.
10. Gorsuch, *On Eagles' Wings*, 60. Schweitzer writes that religious experience was worthwhile before and during combat, but, for most, not relevant during combat, for the obvious reason that during combat one's mind is on other things. See Schweitzer's *Cross and the Trenches*, 132-4.
11. This is not the first study to make this connection but, so far as the authors know, the focus here is original. In *The Acquittal of God: A Theology for Vietnam Veterans* (New York: Pilgrim Press, 1990), Uwe Siemon-Netto writes: "Veterans have often wept when told... that the very essence of the Gospel is that God was suffering with them [in combat]. The God whom they thought of as having gone AWOL in Vietnam turned out to be with them all the way to their cry of dereliction" (74). AWOL = absent without leave.

the point of Jesus' loneliness on the cross was a soldier. "Surely this man was the son of God," said a Roman centurion at Golgotha.[12]

Though the works of a few non-western writers were consulted while research for this manuscript was underway, the examples drawn on here come from westerners (primarily Americans) engaged in the two world wars and the conflicts in Korea, Vietnam, Iraq, and Afghanistan, with the addition of a small sample of memoirs, letters, and diaries from the American Civil War. This study focuses on westerners because the authors feel that they have a general understanding of the western person's mental world. Of course, in English translation, the words of non-westerners, and the sentiments they express, seem familiar. "May God ... come to help my relatives," an Iraqi officer wrote during the Gulf War of 1991. But, then, the officer's cries to Allah seem formulaic and fatalistic. "How I want to see them and find out how they are! God is beneficent. Where are they now? God only knows."[13] Not knowing the culture that shaped these words, the authors are reluctant to come to conclusions. To cite another example: in her wartime diary, the north Vietnamese doctor Dang Thuy Tram writes about the agony war brings to her soul and she often denounces the American "devils" in her country.[14] The language, translated into English, is like that used by American soldiers in Vietnam. But since the culture of Vietnam is foreign to the authors, we focus only on the words of those whose general culture we share.

This study is unusual in that it takes up material from different conflicts without making clear historical distinctions. We do this because, much to our surprise, we found that combat veterans from various theaters of war speak to spiritual concerns in similar ways, though combatants from different conflicts draw on different vocabularies—the ubiquity of the "f" word in post-WWII memoirs being the most notable distinguishing feature. Especially surprising to us were the many similarities between commentary on the American Civil War and twentieth-century conflicts. Sam Watkins' memoir of his time in military service to the Confederacy and Eugene Sledge's account of his combat experience in the Pacific during the Second World War are not as different as one might expect. Still, this study emphasizes the twentieth century because it is personally familiar to readers, and because it is still possible to talk with veterans of most of the United States' twentieth-century conflicts.

While the authors hope that this work will be useful to readers and scholars generally, we should state at the outset (and it may be obvious by now) that we

---

12. Mark 15:39. During the American Civil War, one southern soldier wrote: "Our Redeemer for our sake suffered upon a Roman Cross, and why should not we a degenerate race suffer by the hands of wicked men." See Andrew Carroll, ed., *War Letters: Extraordinary Correspondence from American Wars* (New York: Scribner, 2001), 85.

13. Jon E. Lewis, ed., *War Diaries and Letters: Life on the Battlefield in the Words of the Ordinary Soldier* (New York: Carroll & Graf Publishers, 1999), 488.

14. Dang Thuy Tram, *Last Night I Dreamed of Peace: The Diary of Dang Thuy Tram* trans. Andrew X. Pham (New York: Harmony Books, 2007).

take some basic Christian assumptions for granted and do not explain or defend them. Among our Christian assumptions are: (1) God exists; (2) God interacts with his creation, which includes human beings; (3) given the nature of the Trinity, it is proper to speak of God and Jesus interchangeably; and (4) that, while complicated and often enigmatic, the Bible is a primary source of information about God and his relationship with the world. Finally, because two of the three persons in the Trinity are called father and son, we use the masculine pronoun when speaking of God.

Also, we acknowledge that we have made no attempt to reconcile the violence of the Old Testament's historical books with the message of the Sermon on the Mount and the Gospels generally. Like a lot of things in this complicated life, reconciliation here may not be possible. The First World War poet Wilfred Owen, who ultimately did not survive combat, got at this tension in his poem "Soldier's Dream." He begins by dreaming of a "kind Jesus" who fouls artillery gears and rusts "every bayonet with his tears." But then the Old Testament "God" appears, becomes vexed, and gives all power to Michael the archangel—and the war carries on.[15]

We have talked with war veterans who wanted to reconcile passages in the Old Testament with the Gospels, but it seems to us that they were never able to do so successfully. The deeds of the Christian warrior are sometimes praised but never squared with the command to love one's enemies.[16] What we do know is that the Sermon on the Mount was delivered by Jesus to his disciples. We also know that even the most violent passages in the Old Testament do not justify a "kill them all and let God sort them out" mentality.[17] It seems to be the case that warriors who read the Bible in wartime often avoid biblical tensions by focusing on the comforting Psalms.[18]

15. Wilfred Owen, "Soldier's Dream" in *The Collected Poems of Wilfred Owen*, ed., C. Day Lewis (New York: New Directions Book, 1963), 84.
16. "Jonesy…was as tough a guy as ever mounted the firestep. Jonesy believed in prayer, and he read the Bible, but he could fight, mister!" See Denis, *These Live On*, 65.
17. This view of warfare is expressed in Don Ericson and John L. Rotundo, *Charlie Rangers* (New York: Ivy Books, 1989), 299.
18. Schweitzer, *Cross and the Trenches*, 32-4. A collection of faith-filled testimonials designed to keep up the morale of the American public at the end of the Second World War contains numerous passages from the Bible, all of them from the book of Psalms. See Denis, *These Live On*.

Chapter One

God's Hiddenness in Combat

[E]veryone was just trying to get through it, existential crunch, no atheists in foxholes like you wouldn't believe. Even bitter faith was better than none at all, like the black Marine I'd heard about during heavy shelling...who said, "Don't worry, baby, God'll think of something."
—Michael Herr, journalist, Vietnam

"There are no atheists in foxholes," a veteran says, "or in gun turrets." The turret gunner who asserted this should know. Yet, in the same conversation, he acknowledged that during his Army Air Corps service in the Second World War he did not pray or read the Bible or attend chapel services. Nor did he talk about religious matters with his comrades on their thirty-five bombing missions over Germany. During the war, he said in passing, he was not a Christian.[1] He believed God existed; he had grown up a Baptist. But in wartime he was a practical atheist. For him, God had nothing to do with war.[2] The religion of his childhood did not bring him any special strength.[3]

This veteran's story is common—and veterans who held to their Christian faith through their combat experiences, like those who lost faith or never had it, acknowledge that practicing Christians among combatants are a small minority. Civil War combatants referred to short-lived religious revivals among the troops, but more commonly they observed a general lack of piety. Days set aside for fasting and prayer, for example, were not taken seriously. "We have Christian men in the Regiment," Elisha Hunt Rhodes confided to his diary, "but there

---

1. Second World War veteran in conversation with Preston Jones, Siloam Springs, Arkansas, June 28, 2006. Sam Watkins' memoir of the American Civil War is full of language about heaven and Watkins' hope of meeting his fallen comrades there. Somewhat mysteriously, then, he tells us near the end of the memoir that he "was not a Christian" during the war. See Watkins, *Co Aytch: A Confederate Memoir of the Civil War* (New York: Touchstone, 2003), 224.
2. This is a common sentiment among veterans who identify themselves as Christians and as well as those who do not. In a discussion with another Army Air Corps veteran and prisoner of war in Germany, the veteran said that "God didn't fit" in the world of war. This was the general theme that emerged in the course of interviews with veterans of combat in WWII, Vietnam, and Iraq.
3. Victor Klemperer, a Jew who survived the Second World War while living in Dresden (Eastern Germany) made a similar observation about the Catholicism of a woman he knew. See his *I Will Bear Witness: A Diary of the Nazi Years*, trans. Martin Chalmers (New York: The Modern Library, 2001), 68.

are many who take no interest in religious matters."[4] General Ulysses S. Grant described the last days of the Civil War without even a perfunctory giving of thanks to providence. Grant's only reference to anything religious in his memories surrounding the defeat of the Army of Northern Virginia concerned a church service that was cancelled for the sake of prosecuting battle.[5]

The general theme holds through twentieth century conflicts. A private in the First World War wrote that opportunities "for Christian fellowship were very rare, and under the strain of Army life the Christian soldier often found his spiritual life somewhat at a low ebb."[6] In a last letter home, a German soldier at Stalingrad counted a congregation of eleven at a worship service on Christmas, noting how difficult it had been to find them among the masses of doubting and hopeless men.[7] On the other side of the world, in the American war against the Japanese, one chaplain thought that the attendance of 120 men out of 1,000 at a chapel service seemed unusually good, though he acknowledged that that figure could not approach the numbers that turned out for popular entertainment.[8] Twenty years later, an insightful journalist in Vietnam was struck by the absence of religious devotion among American troops,[9] and a combatant in Vietnam found himself surprised that so many soldiers turned out for a holiday religious service, only then to observe that the troops' piety got lost somewhere on the way to the enlisted men's club.[10] A ten-hour documentary on life aboard an American aircraft carrier devoted one hour to the "faith" of the ship's personnel, but much of this faith was placed in country, friends, and comrades. The religious services depicted were small, representing a tiny fraction of the 5,000 sailors serving on the ship.[11]

Are there atheists in foxholes? One need only consult the literature of, say, the Military Association of Atheists and Freethinkers, or type the well-known

---

4. James Henry Gooding, *On the Altar of Freedom: A Black Soldier's Civil War Letters from the Front* (New York: Warner Books, 1991), 16; Robert Hunt Rhodes, ed., *All for the Union: The Civil War Diary and Letters of Elisha Hunt Rhodes* (New York: Orion, 1985), 71-2. On revival, see Rhodes, 140-1.
5. U.S. Grant, *Personal Memoirs of U.S. Grant* (New York: Da Capo, 1982), 540.
6. Richard Schweitzer, *The Cross and the Trenches: Religious Faith and Doubt among British and American Great War Soldiers* (Westport, CT: Praeger, 2003), 195.
7. Franz Schneider and Charles Gullans, eds. and trans., *Last Letters from Stalingrad* trans., (New York: Signet, 1961), 61.
8. Russell Cartwright Stroup, *Letters from the Pacific: A Combat Chaplain in World War II*, ed., Richard Cartwright Austin (Columbia: University of Missouri Press, 2000), 146 and 159. Stroup reports that another chaplain had an attendance of six soldiers.
9. In *Dispatches* (New York: Vintage International, 1977), Michael Herr writes: "You didn't meet that many who were deeply religious, although you expected to, with so many kids from the South and the Midwest, from farms and small rural towns" (154).
10. Bruce H. Norton, *Force Recon Diary, 1969* (New York: Ivy Books, 1991), 197.
11. *Carrier*, DVD, directed by Maro Chermayeff (Boston: WETA, 2008). This corresponds with the experience of one of this book's authors, Jones, who served aboard the aircraft carrier *U.S.S. Ranger*, 1987-1990.

phrase into an internet search engine to find testimonials from combatants who went into combat as atheists and remained so after the shooting started.[12] Christian combatants who reflect on their war experiences know that there *are* atheists in foxholes. They have seen that if combat drives some men to pray, it also turns church kids into unbelievers.[13] And even though everyone wants to survive, not many are interested in hearing battle-zone sermons on how to gain assurance of eternal life. In one combatant's experience, sermons from evangelical soldiers before patrols were unwelcome, for they assumed that not everyone would survive. And battlefield journalists paint preaching warriors as oddities—less, one gathers, from an anti-Christian bias than from a sense, conscious or not, that combat and Christianity do not go together or, at least, do not seem complementary.[14] "I recognized [during basic training] the incompatibility of religion and the military," recalls Anthony Swofford, an atheist who served in Operation Desert Storm. "The opposite ... seems true when one considers the high number of fiercely religious military people," Swofford continues, "but they are missing something. They're forgetting the mission of the military: to extinguish the lives and livelihood of other humans. What do they think the bombs are for?"[15]

Swofford's formulation—that Christianity and the military are incompatible—is too simple. Yet published and unpublished memoirs of Christian combatants often point to the problematic nature of disciples of the Way, Truth, and Life bringing death and mayhem to others in the context of war.[16] But complete separation of the two is also too simple, for religious language, observations, and metaphors are ubiquitous in memoirs of battle.

To reflect on the place of Christian faith in combat is to be drawn into the complexity—the hellish, bewildering, puzzling, and tangled perplexity—of bat-

---

12. Also see William P. Mahedy, *Out of the Night: The Spiritual Journey of Vietnam Vets* (New York: Ballantine Books, 1986), 127; and Rebecca Phillips, "Beliefwatch: Foxholes" *Newsweek* August 21/28, 2006, 18. In this article, one atheist veteran complains: "Nonbelievers are serving, and have served, in our nation's military with distinction!"

13. See Wallace Terry, *Bloods: An Oral History of the Vietnam War by Black Veterans* (New York: Ballantine Books, 1984): "I guess I got kind of really unreligious because of my Vietnam experience" (30).

14. John Ketwig, *... and a Hard Rain Fell* (Naperville, IL: 2002), 297; and John Sack, *Company C: The Real War in Iraq* (New York: Avon Books, 1995), 6-8, 46-50, 66-7, 93-102, 138, 179-81, 184-9, and 219-21.

15. Anthony Swofford, *Jarhead: A Marine's Chronicle of the Gulf War and Other Battles* (New York: Pocket Books, 2003), 240.

16. Swofford does not specify Christianity in the quotation given above, but it is clear from the context that Christianity—specifically Catholicism—is what he has in mind. The biblical allusion is to John 14:6. In discussions with the authors, two WWII veterans volunteered that combat forced one to break the Sixth Commandment: "Thou shalt not kill" (Exodus 20:13). On the same point see, Sack, *Company C*, 50, 88, 111, 152-3 and 226.

tle itself. It is to look at a world that is unfathomable and is still, in some ways, ordinary. War is a living nightmare where God is not—and is.

Chapter Two

Prayer and Luck

My prayers seem so empty.... With the fog lifting from the water-soaked rice paddies and with wisps of smoke rising from the hooches below us, you'd never guess from high above in our helicopter that a war was going on. Can God actually be in this forgotten place?
—James D. Johnson, combat chaplain, Vietnam

In the Gospels and Christian tradition, prayer has been associated primarily with quiet, solitude, and contemplation. Christian writers refer to prayer as a way of "opening windows to God"; spiritual advisors see prayer as the raising of one's heart to God. Prayer, says one theologian, is "nothing else but an ascending or getting up of the desire of the heart into God by withdrawing it from earthly thoughts." Theologians have suggested that the purpose of prayer is not to force God's will but to find one's own desires conforming to God's. People do not pray "in the hope of changing God's mind, but in order to cooperate with Him in bringing about certain effects which He has foreordained."[1] The Christian's ideal is to pray without ceasing in order to allow God to fill each moment with his presence.

Over time, prayer in the West became increasingly personalized and came frequently to include praise, thanksgiving, and appeals to saints. Some came to see that prayer is not a one-way form of communication but should involve listening for God's guidance. Thomas Merton suggests that there are "no tricks and no shortcuts" in the spiritual life, for it requires deliberate and disciplined meditation. Henri Nouwen writes that the spiritual life is impossible without solitude, which is necessary to quiet the "inner chaos" and outside distractions of life.[2]

Thomas Aquinas, among the most important theologians in Christian history, wrote that prayer requires several qualities. He claimed that a prayer should, first of all, be confident because Christ is the Christian's advocate. And prayer should be ordered, meaning that one places spiritual interests before earthly ones. Prayer, Aquinas continued, should be suitable—in the words of St. John Damascene, "asking [for] what is right and appropriate from God." And

---

1. See "Prayer" in *Concise Oxford Dictionary of the Christian Church* ed., E. A. Livingstone (New York: Oxford University Press, 2006); and Richard J. Foster and James Bryan Smith, eds. *Devotional Classics: Selected Readings for Individuals and Groups* (San Francisco: HarperSanFrancisco, 1993), 101-5.
2. Foster, *Devotional Classics*, 67, 80-4. Also see C.S. Lewis, *The Joyful Christian* (New York: Collier Books, 1977), 89-90.

prayer should be devout, because "piety makes the sacrifice of prayer acceptable to God" and arises from love for others. Finally, prayer should be humble because all good things come from God.[3]

Given this, and given the fact that combat is not conducive to philosophical solitude and the opening of oneself to the divine, one wonders if prayer can have any place in the moment of battle. Of course, the obvious response to the query is that, in the world of war, prayer of some kind is everywhere. One Civil War combatant observed, as have many since, that guns seem more useful in war than prayer, but this does not prevent the offering of supplications to anything that can help.[4]

As warriors did in earlier conflicts, wounded American soldiers in Vietnam inter-mixed appeals to God, the Virgin Mary, and their mothers.[5] In his battle-tide prayers one Cobra pilot "took unto himself Jesus, Jehovah, Buddha, Mohammed, Moses, St. Cecilia, [and] the Blessed Virgin." He could just as easily have prayed to Elvis or to an Indian monkey god.[6] Meanwhile, and more seriously, we envision a sergeant taking a dead Marine in his arms and crying, "Please, God, don't take this one. Let me keep this one,"[7] while another infantryman prays, clenching his teeth and cursing the enemy.[8] One chaplain who recognized that warriors might see prayer as an expression of fear, offered petitions among them in the form of jokes and chatter.[9] Another chaplain wrote in his diary, "I have prayed each day and night for peace in my personal war. God, where are you?"[10]

Some young men write to their families reminding them to pray—because prayer "makes a difference."[11] Others, such as an atheist Marine serving in the Middle East, are the unwitting subjects of prayers from believing family mem-

3. Mary T. Clark, ed., *An Aquinas Reader* (New York: Fordham University Press, 1972), 528-30.
4. William A. Fletcher, *Rebel Private: Front and Rear* (New York: Meridian, 1997), 115.
5. James R. McDonough, *Platoon Leader: A Memoir of Command in Combat* (New York: Ballantine Books, 1985), 101; and Ben Sherman, *Medic! The Story of a Conscientious Objector in the Vietnam War* (New York: Writer's Club Press, 2002), 91.
6. Denis Marvicsin, *Maverick: The Personal War of a Vietnam Cobra Pilot* (New York: Jove Books, 1996), 272.
7. William H. Hardwick, *Down South: One Tour in Vietnam* (New York: Ballantine Books, 2002), 38.
8. E.B. Sledge, *With the Old Breed: At Peleliu and Okinawa* (New York: Oxford University Press, 1981). 63.
9. Russell Cartwright Stroup, *Letters from the Pacific: A Combat Chaplain in World War II*, ed., Richard Cartwright Austin (Columbia: University of Missouri Press, 2000), 75.
10. Johnson, *Combat Chaplain: A Thirty-Year Vietnam Battle* (Denton, TX: University of North Texas Press, 2001), 14 and 82.
11. Byron E. Holley, *Vietnam, 1968-1969: A Battalion Surgeon's Journal* (New York: Ivy Books, 1993), 32.

bers.[12] The 23rd Psalm was a battlefield prayer said by one fighter who thanked God that a comrade's mother would never see what had happened to her dead and mangled son.[13] A chaplain prayed for the family of a dead soldier yet to receive the bad news.[14]

The prayers of combatants are usually simple and to the point. One combatant in Vietnam cries, "God, please watch over me,"[15] and another, sitting in the back of a helicopter under enemy fire, promises that he will quit smoking and stay away from whorehouses if God keeps him alive.[16] Elsewhere, an army mechanic thanked God that he never went into battle,[17] and a combat nurse prayed that the mercy she showed to a wounded enemy would be reciprocated elsewhere in the world of war. Years later, she still prayed for a wounded Vietnamese boy nicknamed Baby Huey. "If he's still alive," she says to God, "bless him."[18] A German soldier fighting the Russians counted the blessing that came to him in the form of only a minor wound.[19]

In a combat zone you pray that the battle will be over quickly, that the incoming artillery will stop, that you will die without screaming, and that God will make the nightmare go away.[20] On your helmet you sarcastically write "Pray for war," or you send up an ironic missive: "Just You and Me God, Right?"[21] You utter a word of thanks for America;[22] you believe that your mother's prayers, which seem to be more important than anyone else's, will protect you from the

---

12. Joel Turnipseed, *Baghdad Express: A Gulf War Memoir* (New York: Penguin Books, 2003), 117.

13. Sledge, *With the Old Breed*, 79.

14. Johnson, *Combat Chaplain*, 108.

15. Ches Schneider, *From Classrooms to Claymores: A Teacher at War in Vietnam* (New York: Ivy Books, 1999), 40. Also see, Andrew Exum, *This Man's Army: A Soldier's Story from the Front Lines of the War on Terrorism* (New York: Gotham, 2005), 99.

16. Robert Mason, *Chickenhawk: A Shattering Account of the Helicopter War in Vietnam* (New York: Penguin Books, 1983), 180. A soldier in WWI similarly promised to remain faithful to his wife in exchange for God's protection. See Schweitzer, *Cross and the Trenches: Religious Faith and Doubt among British and American Great War Soldiers* (Westport, CT: Praeger, 2003), 130.

17. John Ketwig, *... and a Hard Rain Fell: A GI's True Story of the War in Vietnam* (Naperville, IL: Sourcebooks, 2002),, 219.

18. Lynn Hampton, *The Fighting Strength: Memoirs of a Combat Nurse in Vietnam* (New York: Warner Books, 1990), 75 and 93.

19. Siefried Knappe with Ted Brusaw, *Soldat: Reflections of a German Soldier, 1936-1949* (New York: Dell Publishing, 1992), 183.

20. Sledge, *With the Old Breed*, 49; Philip Caputo, *A Rumor of War* (New York: Henry Holt, 1977), 272; Schneider, *Classrooms to Claymores*, 69; Ben Sherman, *Medic! The Story of a Conscientious Objector in the Vietnam War* (Lincoln, NB: Writers Club Press, 2002), 187.

21. Michael Herr, *Dispatches* (New York: Vintage International, 1977), 27 and 74.

22. Holley, *Vietnam*, 24

enemy.[23] In battle you thank God that the enemy does not have napalm,[24] and you hear leaders say that the prayers of family members resonate in "the hearts" of the troops.[25] Prayer is bargaining, an "insurance policy," but only for the living. An enemy soldier prays to Jesus or Buddha—perhaps both—but he is still incinerated.[26]

Soldiers' prayers are written, practiced, rehearsed, and (in Vietnam) printed on a plastic-coated card from the Defense Department. But the combat warrior's prayer is difficult to explain—it is "translated outside of language, into chaos—screams, begging, promises, threats, sobs, repetitions of holy names until...throats [are] cracked dry."[27] A warrior feels guilt for praying that God will help him kill well, but he prays it anyway.[28] Later he says, "My God, what have we done? ... Please God, forgive us."[29]

Prayers join artillery and bullets and shrieks in the air:

> Prayers in the Delta, prayers in the Highlands, prayers in the marine bunkers of the "frontier" facing the [demilitarized zone], and for every prayer there was a counter-prayer—it was hard to see who had the edge. In Dalat the emperor's mother sprinkled rice in her hair so the birds could fly around her and feed while she said her morning prayers. In wood-paneled, air-conditioned chapels in Saigon...padres would fire one up to sweet muscular Jesus, blessing ammo dumps and 105's and officers' clubs. The best-armed patrols in history went out after services to feed smoke to people whose priests could let themselves burn down to consecrated ash on street corners. Deep in the valleys you could hear small Buddhist chimes ringing for peace.[30]

---

23. See Hampton, *The Fighting Strength*, acknowledgements; Thomas R. O'Brien, *Blessings from the Battlefield* (Huntington, IN: Our Sunday Visitor Publishing, 2002), 98; and Stroup, *Letters from the Pacific*, 17.

24. Holley, *Vietnam,*66.

25. President George H.W. Bush reflecting on the Gulf War in its immediate aftermath, recorded in *Desert Storm: The Victory*, VHS Turner Home Entertainment (1991).

26. McDonald, *Into the Green: A Reconnaissance By Fire* (New York: Plume, 2001), 19. Also see Caputo, *Rumor of War*. Caputo writes: "[W]e see the Viet Cong behind the dike sitting up with his arms outstretched, in the pose of a man beseeching God. He seems to be pleading for mercy from the screaming mass of technology that is flying no more than one hundred feet above him. But the plane...fires its cannon...and blasts him to shreds" (298).

27. Herr, *Dispatches*, 58.

28. Caputo, *Rumor of War*, 264.

29. Ibid., 321. Also see John Sack, *Company C: The Real War in Iraq* (New York: Avon Books, 1995), 162, 195 and 204-5; and Joshua Lawrence Chamberlain, *The Passing of the Armies* (New York: Barnes and Noble, 2004), 194.

30. Herr, *Dispatches,* 45.

Sometimes one prays even for the enemy—that they will be blessed or that they will see the folly of their ways.[31] "I pray daily," a Marine said after the fact, "for everyone I had to kill in Vietnam."[32] A Jewish convert to Catholicism prayed for Hitler because even that dictator had an immortal soul.[33]

But is the combatant's life in God's hands or the Grim Reaper's?[34] When shrapnel is flying, is life and death a matter of providence or fate or fortune or chance or cosmic coincidence or the inevitable?[35]

In battle, or when they are being tortured in prisoner of war camps, men call out "Jesus!" but it is not clear if the cry is a supplication or a curse or a grasping after good fortune.[36] A friend cries, "Oh God, I'm hit!" and you do not know if that has as much (or more) to do with the recognition of expended luck as with a glimpse into eternity.[37] A warrior says, "I prayed hard for a chopper to come and get me away from there," but the same meaning could have been conveyed if he had said that he had hoped or wished.[38] "This time all the luck in the world was with us," writes another. "We wished him luck.... We hoped our luck would hold out.... We had received a lucky hit."[39]

Providence, Lady Luck, fate, the odds, a roll of the dice—in combat memoirs the concepts are usually interchangeable: "Would my luck hold out?" a warrior asks, and then begins to pray the 23rd Psalm while squeezing his rifle.[40] "I became fatalistic," writes another, "praying only for my fate to be painless."[41] A soldier in Europe was grateful to providence for his luck in not being hit by artillery shells.[42] Elisha Hunt Rhodes, fighting for the Union in the Civil War, wrote repeatedly in his diary about the good protection of providence, but usually just to the extent that that protection pertained to him. He had less to say, or pray, concerning providence and the lives of his close comrades; he prayed for him-

---

31. Sack, *Company C*, 138. In *Desert Storm: The Victory*, a soldier is recorded saying that he was praying for himself and U.S. forces and then curtly added that he had also prayed for the Iraqis.
32. Thomas O'Brien, *Blessings from the Battlefield*, 68. Johnson, *Combat Chaplain*, prayed for the families of killed Vietcong (43 and 54).
33. Victor Klemperer, *I Will Bear Witness: A Diary of the Nazi Years*, trans. Martin Chalmers (New York: The Modern Library, 2001), 450.
34. McDonough, *Platoon Leader,* 69.
35. "Over us, Chance hovers," writes Erich Maria Remarque, *All Quiet on the Western Front* (New York: Random House, 1982), 101. And see Marvicsin, *Maverick*, 113; Gary Linderer, *Six Silent Men: 101st LRP/Rangers* vol. III (New York: Ivy Books, 1997), 97; Johnson, *Combat Chaplain*, 201; Klemperer, *I Will Bear Witness*, 289.
36. Eric Lomax, *The Railway Man: A True Story of War, Remembrance, and Forgiveness* (New York: Ballantine Books, 1995), 120. And see Sledge, *With the Old Breed*, 67, 69.
37. Sledge, *With the Old Breed*, 111; and Marvicsin, *Maverick*, 89.
38. Herr, *Dispatches*, 122.
39. George Wilson, *If You Survive* (New York: Ivy Books, 1987), 60, 67 and 93.
40. Sledge, *With the Old Breed,* 111. Also see Knappe, *Soldat*, 204 and 248-9.
41. Sledge, *With the Old Breed*, 147.
42. Wilson, *If You Survive*, 168.

self and a nebulous "us." He saw too much of the randomness of war to hope
that his close associates would make it through.[43]

So a soldier wonders: what is greater, God or fate?[44] Is surviving a close
call the work of luck, divine guidance, blind chance, fortune, or an act of providence?[45] One day a combat surgeon reflected on fate as the true hunter of men;
the next day he credited life and death to the Lord.[46] "The general had said our
success was due to Preparation and Luck," a chaplain wrote in 1944. "I re-
minded the men that, for us, 'luck' was a poor description of God."[47]

Sometimes combatants think they can gain God's favor by carrying Bibles
("Gideons in fatigues"), crosses, crucifixes, and saints' images as good luck
charms.[48] The British corporal E. Foulkes, in the First World War, supersti-
tiously sang the hymn "Jesus, Lover of my soul" for hours on end, until he
"could only croak the words."[49] In a crunch, Protestants may clamor for rosa-
ries.[50] But it is not obvious that these sacred pieces of fortune are superior to
locks of a friend's hair, a tiger's claw, a rabbit foot, a piece of string tied around
one's wrist, strips of a lover's underwear, pictures of family, friends, pets, and
rock stars, or lucky flight suits.[51] The important thing is to believe in *something*,
a career veteran says—"family, God, whatever."[52] "[W]e've got everything
here," said a soldier in Vietnam to a new guy. "Jews, Catholics, Protestants,

----

43. Robert Hunt Rhodes, ed., *All for the Union: The Civil War Diary and Letters of Elisha Hunt Rhodes* (New York: Orion, 1985), 56, 59, 60, 62, 87, 88, 205.
44. Franz Schneider and Charles Gullans, eds. and trans., *Last Letters from Stalingrad*
trans., (New York: Signet, 1961), 121.
45. Holley, *Vietnam*, 96; Caputo, *Rumor of War*, 281; Edwin Campion Vaughan, *Some
Desperate Glory: The World War One Diary of a British Officer* (New York: Henry Holt,
1990), 34 and 38; Sledge, *With the Old Breed*, 218.
46. Holley, *Vietnam*, 75.
47. Stroup, *Letters from the Pacific*, 193. Also see Johnson, *Combat Chaplain*: "This
fatalistic attitude is very poor theology and reflects a kind of predestined attitude that
people have begun to voice here in Vietnam" (80). In his study of combatants in the Second World War, Gerald Linderman saw that soldiers who petitioned God did not hesitate
simultaneously to solicit luck. See Linderman's *World within War: America's Combat
Experience in World War II* (Cambridge: Harvard University Press, 1997), 66.
48. Herr, *Dispatches*, 57. On "Gideons in fatigues" see Turnipseed, *Baghdad Express*, 82.
49. Schweitzer, *Cross and the Trenches*, 21.
50. Thomas O'Brien, *Blessings from the Battlefield*, 44.
51. Herr, *Dispatches*, 57; Exum, *This Man's Army*, xii; and Marvicsin, *Maverick*, 51 and
158.
52. In *If I Die in a Combat Zone: Box Me Up and Ship Me Home* (New York: Dell Publishing, 1969), Tim O'Brien remembers a chaplain saying that, questions of God aside,
"there's still faith and you have to have it. You've got to have faith in somebody" (65).
John McCain, a POW in Vietnam, writes about the "three essential keys to resistance:
faith in God, country, and fellow prisoners." See McCain, *Faith of My Fathers* (New
York: Random House, 1999), 252.

atheists, and at least one Baptist. Use whatever works."[53] Belief gets you through. The particular object of belief is not really important.[54]

Battle-tide prayers can bring comfort. It seems plausible that the ability to "dial up God" in times of stress can give one a psychological edge on the enemy.[55] But prayers for survival, or the prayer that one can be spared having to kill, are superseded by prayers for the family of a dead comrade and by supplications for mercy after killing has been done. In combat you can toss up a prayer for protection and success to The Man Upstairs, but you know that wars are won by soldiers, whether or not they pray. "If plans are sensible and orders are followed, religion has no bearing on the outcome of battle."[56] A soldier in the First World War asked why God should pay attention to his particular prayers. "There's people being killed all around me," he wrote. "Why should [God] save my life?"[57]

In the context of battle, there is an understandable grasping for straws. From ancient times prayers have been said for the protection of combatants, but some do not return home.[58] Survivors know that their dead comrades had also said their prayers; they had carried their good luck charms; they had believed that they would see their families again.[59] Prayer is no guarantee. "You could make all the ritual moves, carry your lucky piece, wear your magic jungle hat, [or] kiss your thumb knuckle smooth as stones under running water," a combat journalist writes, but "the Inscrutable Immutable was still out there, and you kept on or not at its pitiless discretion."[60] The researchers asked combat veterans: why did *you* survive? Many said, simply, that they do not know.[61]

---

53. Joseph T. Ward, *Dear Mom: A Sniper's Vietnam* (New York: Ivy Books, 1991), 9.

54. On the ecumenical spirit on the Western Front during World War I, see Schweitzer, *Cross and the Trenches*, 69-71.

55. Jack Coughlin and Casey Kuhlman with Donald A. Davis, *Shooter: The Autobiography of the Top-Ranked Marine Sniper* (New York: St. Martin's Paperbacks, 2005), 86.

56. Billy Waugh with Tim Keown, *Hunting the Jackal: A Special Forces and CIA Soldier's Fifty Years on the Frontlines of the War against Terrorism* (New York: Avon Books, 2004), 30 and 145. For useful reflections on prayer and contingency, see John Polkinghorne, *Science and Providence: God's Interaction with the World* (Boston: Shambhala Publications, 1989), 69-76.

57. Schweitzer, *Cross and the Trenches*, 202

58. For example, at the beginning of the Boer War a Canadian prayed "to the God of armies and of justice, begging that he spare [Canadian] lives." See Gaston P. Labat, *Le Livre d'Or of the Canadian Contingents in South Africa* (Montreal, 1901), 33.

59. Sledge, *With the Old Breed,* imagined a dead Marine saying to him: "I prayed like you to survive, but look at me now" (270)

60. Herr, *Dispatches*, 56.

61. Among the many who have said this in conversations with the authors was a WWII veteran, the only survivor of a group of 25 fighter pilots. He was ordered to remain stateside; his 24 comrades were killed when their transport ship was attacked and sunk in the Pacific.

Chapter Three

Combat and Christian Symbols

The chaplain ... was seriously undermining my faith in God.... Hearing that man say that Jesus wanted me to be in Afghanistan ending the lives of fellow humans was too much for my faith to handle at the time. I preferred to think that what I was doing was outside God's will, and rather one of life's ugly realities.
—Andrew Exum, soldier, Afghanistan

In wartime, prayer and luck, piety and superstition, spiritual devotion and dedication to country can be confused—or they can merge and mix. Vera Brittain wrote about Oxford during the First World War: "In the churches..., where so many of the congregation are soldiers, we are always having it impressed upon us that 'the call of country is the call of God.'" [1] This kind of conflation of interests is common. Writers tell us about a Marine chapel with stained glass windows depicting the flag-raising at Iwo Jima and a warrior operating a flame thrower,[2] and about a chaplain giving a sermon on the Marines' nickname, "Devil Dog." Jesus was the first Devil Dog, said the chaplain, the "Devil Dog you will want on your side going into battle."[3]

Perhaps for more than any other Christian symbol, the meaning of the cross has altered and morphed. For the Romans, the cross pointed to a humiliating and agonizing death meted to slaves and non-citizens. The cross was for criminals and the lowly. When Jesus called on his disciples to take up their cross and follow him, he was speaking not only about a burden his followers were to carry, but about the willingness to face wrenching public shame and the possibility, literally, of excruciating death.[4] Because of its connotations, the earliest Christian communities did not use the cross as a positive symbol except to stir a bold identification with Christ's sufferings. In the early second century, Ignatius of Antioch praised the steadfastness of persecuted Christians who were in the process of being made perfect "in an unshakable faith, like people nailed to the cross of our Lord Jesus Christ both in the flesh and in the spirit."[5]

---

1. Vera Brittain, *Testament of Youth: One Woman's Haunting Record of the First World War* (New York: Penguin Books, 1989), 127.
2. Thomas Ricks, *Making the Corps* (New York: Simon and Schuster, 1997), 116.
3. Evan Wright, *Generation Kill: Devil Dogs, Iceman, Captain America, and the New Face of American War* (New York: G.P. Putnam's Sons, 2004), 47.
4. See, for example, Mark 8:34.
5. J. Robert Wright, ed., *Readings for the Daily Office from the Early Church* (New York: Church Publishing Incorporated, 1991), 25.

By the fourth century, Christians had appropriated the cross as a sometimes positive symbol and the crucifix came to mean more than the wretchedness of execution. Crucifixes came to be used for promoting devotion, and the cross inspired sacred feasts, liturgical veneration, and individual adoration.[6] Churches weaved the sign of the cross into artwork to inspire piety, or to symbolize the life, fruitfulness, and unity of the Christian way. Like some modern warriors, medieval churches used the cross as a talisman against demons, and religious figures incorporated the cross into their coats of arms to represent their oneness with Christ, just as some modern combatants wear crosses and crucifixes as necklaces or tattoos.

The meanings of the cross in pre-modern times were various. Irenaeus, Bishop of Lyon, wrote that Christ's "obedience on the tree of the cross reversed the disobedience at the tree in Eden." Leo the Great, Bishop of Rome, reveled in the "power of the cross," the "supremacy of Christ crucified," and Christ's experience on the cross as an "example which leads us to generosity." Cyril, Bishop of Jerusalem, said that the cross was the Church's "supreme glory." The "cross used to denote punishment," wrote John Chrysostom in the early fourth century, "but it has now become a focus of glory. It was formerly a symbol of condemnation but it is now seen as a principle of salvation."[7]

In one of the great reverses of symbolic history, the cross changed from a symbol of disgrace to one of conquest. According to legend, St. George, the patron saint of England, fought the dragon of Libya under the sign of the cross, and his victory over the serpent led to both the conversion of a town and to the cross' place on England's flag. In the early fourth century, the Roman emperor Constantine fought the Battle of the Milvian Bridge after seeing a vision of the cross and hearing a voice saying *in hoc signo vinces* ("by this sign you shall conquer"). The crusaders famously fought "for the Cross,"[8] and some of them supposedly took a portion of the True Cross with them into battle, where it was captured by Saladin and used to barter for an exchange of prisoners in 1191.[9] Before the battle at Agincourt, Henry V and his army heard Mass three times and took communion; his soldiers made the sign of the cross and took "earth into their mouths as a symbolic gesture of the death and burial they were thereby accepting."[10]

---

6. The Decree of the Seventh Ecumenical Council of Nicaea (787 A.D.) stated that "the figure of the precious and life-giving Cross," along with other objects (such as the Gospels, incense, and lights), could be used to help worshipers focus their minds on the eternal things these objects represented or pointed to. See Wright, *Readings for the Daily Office*, 59.

7. Wright, *Readings for the Daily Office*, 11, 129, 136, 163, 209.

8. John Keegan, *A History of Warfare* (New York: Vintage Books, 1994), 290-1.

9. John Carey, ed., *Eyewitness to History* (New York: Avon Books, 1987), 35-7.

10. John Keegan, *Face of Battle* (New York: Viking Press, 1976), 114. In a contemporary account of the battle, a French knight states that Henry's army spent most of a day "engaged in devotional exercises, praying our Lord God that he would be their help," and

In modern times, western militaries have adopted crosses as meritorious medals. In the First World War, Adolph Hitler received a first and second class Iron Cross, as well as a third class Military Cross.[11] The American hero Eddie Rickenbacker received the Croix de Guerre.[12] The cross symbolized skill and valor in combat; it rewarded killing. At the same time, the graves of warriors killed in combat were marked with crosses.[13] So the cross came to symbolize both having killed well and having been killed. We further notice that, in 1863, the International Committee of the Red Cross adopted its symbol on a white background as its universal mark. Here the cross pointed to neutrality, protection, and medical care.

Religious symbols, like prayer, are everywhere in combat because religion is everywhere in combat, because combat—preparation for it and the execution and commemoration of it—takes on the elements of a religion. No one is surprised when the drill instructor at basic training says that your soul may belong to Jesus, but everything else belongs to the Marines.[14] No one is amazed when a memoirist calls drill instructors high priests for military novitiates.[15] We are not shocked that a recruit learns that rifles are holy things and that the Marine Corps' symbols are "God-holy icons."[16] We can understand that following an exact personal regimen before battle or cleaning one's rifle can become a "ritual" and the repetition of *fire* as a comrade discharges his weapon can be some-

---

during the night "all that could find a priest confessed themselves." See Carey, *Eyewitness to History*, 68-9.

11. John Toland, *Adolph Hitler* vol. I (Garden City, NY: Doubleday, 1976), 74.

12. Edward V. Rickenbacker, *Fighting the Flying Circus* (New York: Frederick A. Stokes Co., 1919), 70-1.

13. Brittain, *Testament of Youth*, 144.

14. E. B. Sledge, *With the Old Breed: At Peleliu and Okinawa* (New York: Oxford University Press, 1981), 8. Religious language punctuates the basic training portion of *Full Metal Jacket*, VHS, directed by Stanley Kubrick (New York, NY: Warner Home Video, 1987). Vietnam veterans interviewed by the authors say that this film is generally accurate. In the film one sees, among many other things germane to this study, a recruit punched by the drill instructor for saying that he does not believe in the Virgin Mary.

15. Philip Caputo, *A Rumor of War* (New York: Henry Holt, 1977), 8. In *Jarhead: A Marine's Chronicle of the Gulf War and Other Battles* (New York: Pocket Books, 2003), Anthony Swofford puts flesh and bones on this. "At boot camp," he writes, "I was chosen Catholic lay reader. When all the Catholic recruits had been herded into one corner of the squad bay, I was within arm's reach of Drill Instructor Seats, who grabbed me by my collar and said, 'You, fuckface, you're the goddamn Catholic lay reader. Whenever a Catholic recruit wants to pray, you lead the fucking prayer. If a Catholic recruit wants a goddamn Bible, you shit him a Bible, pronto.... There really isn't a Catholic prayer every night, except the one your drill instructors tell about praying that you shitbag recruits become mean, green killing motherfuckers. On Sundays, you march this shit bucket of Catholics over to the church.... [A]ny time your drill instructors decide it's time for the Catholics to pray, you better shit me a prayer, do you understand fuckface?'" (238-9).

16. Sledge, *With the Old Breed,* vii; Swofford, *Jarhead*, 181. Swofford calls dogtags "icons" (240).

thing like a "religious chant."[17] (One veteran says: "We, as mere human beings made of flesh, blood, thought, dreams, prayer, and spit absorb power and energy from the machines we use.")[18]

And so it goes. Hungry soldiers gather around a table of food as if it were an altar.[19] First combat is said to be one's baptism into a living death, "that soldier's sacrament."[20] A soldier refers to the protective blasts from his machine gun as "Jesus fire"—that is, bullets from friendly troops above protecting comrades in a valley below.[21] Another writes that any patrol or mission can suddenly turn into "the worst chapter of the book of Revelation" and that enemy fire sometimes pours in like donations to TV preachers.[22] A different memoirist says that the sound of helicopters coming to the rescue is like God's voice from the heavens.[23] To have the power of dealing life and death in battle is to be godlike.[24]

After first combat, when the romance of war is gone, some soldiers about to go on patrol attend chapel services and Mass while others gamble.[25] Before battle more warriors pray and go to chapel than usual;[26] if no chaplain is near, they might create makeshift churches of their own: "just a few guys stood around

17. Sledge, *With the Old Breed*, 37; Swofford, *Jarhead*, 188; and Andrew Exum, *This Man's Army: A Soldier's Story from the Front Lines of the War on Terrorism* (New York: Gotham, 2005), xii.

18. Cherokee Paul McDonald, *Into the Green: A Reconnaissance by Fire* (New York: Plume, 2001), 143.

19. Erich Maria Remarque, *All Quiet on the Western Front* (New York: Random House, 1982), 234.

20. Caputo, *Rumor of War*, 72. One nurse's "baptism" into the realities of combat was gas mask training. See Lynn Hampton, *Fighting Strength: Memoirs of a Combat Nurse in Vietnam* (New York: Warner Books, 1990), 13.

21. Exum, *This Man's Army*, 167.

22. Denis Marvicsin, *Maverick: The Personal War of a Vietnam Cobra Pilot* (New York: Jove Books, 1996), 36 and 173.

23. Billy Waugh, *Hunting the Jackal: A Special Forces and CIA Soldier's Fifty Years on the Frontlines of the War against Terrorism* (New York: Avon, 2004), 107.

24. John L. Rotundo and Don Ericson, *Charlie Rangers* (New York: Ivy Books, 1989), 7.

25. See the introduction to *The Anderson Platoon*, Public Video (1996).

26. In *A Table in the Presence* (Nashville: W Publishing Group, 2002), Carey Cash observed the heightened religiosity of Marines on the point of entering combat and interpreted it as genuine religious revival. Also see Russell Cartwright Stroup, *Letters from the Pacific: A Combat Chaplain in World War II*, ed., Richard Cartwright Austin (Columbia: University of Missouri Press, 2000). Stroup writes that the belief that men approaching combat attend services only from fear was a "libel" on them (111). And see Siegfried Knappe and Ted Brusaw, *Soldat: Reflections of a German Soldier, 1936-1949* (New York: Dell Publishing, 1992), 204; William A. Fletcher, *Rebel Private, Front and Rear: Memoirs of a Confederate Soldier* (New York: Meridian, 1997), 78; and Karl Zinmeister, *Boots on the Ground: A Month with the 82nd Airborne in the Battle for Iraq* (New York: St. Martin's, 2004), 32.

twigs tied together to form a cross. We would say a prayer, and then do last minute busywork for the mission."[27]

Religious language permeates the world of war. The fundamental creed of the combat zone is that a soldier or Marine can rely on his buddy,[28] and warriors pray that they will not let their buddies down; combatants vow never to leave a comrade behind.[29] The battle-wounded count on miracle-working medics; hospitals seem like sacred places; and in the combat surgeon's operating room, one feels as if he is doing "priestly work."[30] Survivors of the gunfire, bombs, sleeplessness, hunger, pests, weather, fear, and randomness see the fear of death lose its sting to indifference,[31] though they still pray for lost buddies.[32] To be assigned a rear echelon job after months in a combat zone is to have received "salvation."[33] One warrior likens the environment of war to a church:

> You do not want to go clanking and grunting along the center aisle between the pews, draped in your vestments of death, propelled by your desire to reach the altar. No. You wish to sit and reflect, gather your thoughts, give thanks for your breath, wrap yourself in quiet, open your senses to receive the Word, and wait....[The enemy's] stealthy feet tread across and upon the Word with arrogant ignorance, and when they finally, hesitantly, come into range of your ministry you bless them with a fire-and-brimstone sermon aimed at teaching them the folly of life and the certainty of death.[34]

In combat, the facts of war and religious mission get mixed up. A soldier in Vietnam scribbled "Kill a gook for God" on his helmet,[35] and Chaplain Carey Cash wrote that "the God of the Bible is a God who fights for what is right, a God who contends with those who plot evil against His own"—the "right" being whatever the U.S. government decides to do with its military, "His own" being the U.S. Marines: for, as Cash tells us, "God has the heart of an infantryman."[36]

---

27. Ches Schneider, *From Classrooms to Claymores: A Teacher at War in Vietnam* (New York: Ivy Books, 1999), 183.

28. Sledge, *With the Old Breed,* 108.

29. This is a major theme of *Black Hawk Down*, Columbia TriStar Home Entertainment (2002), which exemplified this basic point of the Army Rangers' Creed.

30. Byron E. Holley, *Vietnam, 1968-1969: A Battalion Surgeon's Journal* (New York: Ivy Books, 1993), foreword; Hampton, *Fighting Strength,* 85; Ben Sherman, *Medic! The Story of a Conscientious Objector in the Vietnam War* (New York: Writer's Club Press, 2002), 80.

31. Caputo, *Rumor of War,* 260. The allusion is to I Corinthians 15:55.

32. Michael Herr, *Dispatches* (New York: Vintage International, 1977), 23.

33. Tim O'Brien, *If I Die in a Combat Zone, Box Me Up and Ship Me Home* (New York: Dell Publishing, 1973),171.

34. McDonald, *Into the Green,* 140.

35. *Vietnam: A Television History, VHS, vol x,* directed by Matthew Collins and Rocky Collins (Boston: WGBH, 1993).

36. Cash, *Table in the Presence,* 215 and 222.

Cash's stark conflation of Christian belief and military doctrine is unusual, but its sharp-toothed, Old Testament, Canaanite-slaying, emotion-driven, martial religiosity fits the world of war.[37] The journalist Michael Herr described the conflict in Vietnam as:

> Holy war, long-nosed jihad like a face-off between one god who would hold the coonskin to the wall while we nailed it up, and another whose detachment would see the blood run out of ten generations, if that was how long it took for the wheel to go around.[38]

Philip Caputo draws on the language of liturgy:

> Evening vespers began at seven o'clock, when the howitzers and mortars started firing their routine harassment missions.... The platoon rose as one, like a congregation at a Mass.... The commands were not really necessary. They were just part of the ritual.[39]

Some Nazis, too, construed their depredations as holy war.[40]

***

The appropriation of religious language in combat memoirs comes primarily in figures of speech and passing remarks. Except when considering the words of memoirists such as Caputo, who draws on his Catholic education to describe what he felt and saw in combat, one is reluctant to read too much into them. Western speech has long made use of biblical and theological language.[41] Yet it seems that the words of Sunday school, theology, sermons, and the Bible appear too much in combatants' memoirs to pass over as the stuff only of metaphor.

Somehow, in some way, it seems that war *is* religious, for combat engages the soul—it affects the deepest parts of the human psyche—it provides its agents with rituals and primary loyalties. In war, concern for eternal life is trumped by the desire to survive the combat mission. The belief that God loves the world and wants to save it is superseded by prayers of thanks that my buddy, my platoon, or I myself survived the bombardment or the barrage or the ambush. Lov-

---

37. See Richard Marcinko, *Rogue Warrior* (New York: Pocket Star Books), 1992, where we read that, for the author, God is an underwater demolition team leader, among other things (106-8).
38. Herr, *Dispatches*, 45.
39. Caputo, *Rumor of War*, 234 and 252.
40. Victor Klemperer, *I Will Bear Witness: A Diary of the Nazi Years*, trans. Martin Chalmers (New York: The Modern Library, 2001), 343.
41. For example, in 1931 a member of Australia's Labor party denounced an economic policy in the following terms: "[A]re we justified in spitting upon the altar of Labor simply because others may desecrate it worse than we may? That is not the path of salvation...this Government is crucifying the very people who raised its members from obscurity and placed them in power." In Frank Welsh, *Australia: A New History of the Great Southern Land* (New York: The Overlook Press, 2004), 399.

ing your neighbor in a sense congruent with the Sermon on the Mount and the letters of St. John is impossible: a chaplain acknowledged that love of an enemy is not an easy topic to discuss among warriors.[42] The love of God in a personal sense is suspended, replaced by duty, loyalty, the job, the cause, the well-being of the guy next to you. The household of believers is replaced by the great brotherhood of warriors.[43]

Among combatants, the language of faith is ubiquitous. Marines die, kill, and recover from wounds—they remain true to the commands of their superiors and to their nation—while "keeping the faith." Prisoners of war credit their survival to faith in country and family.[44] Soldiers foster or lose faith in their government's cause.[45] Toward the end of the Second World War many Germans put their faith in promised miracle weapons that never materialized or were ineffective.[46] The Confederate survivor Sam Watkins wrote of his dead comrades as having "died for the faith that each state was a separate sovereign government."[47]

So war, in some way, is religious; it is a vehicle of complicated faith.[48] Yet combat is also a spiritual black hole. Prayer and religious language are everywhere in the combat zone. Is God?

---

42. Stroup, *Letters from the Pacific*, 60. Also see William P. Mahedy, *Out of the Night: The Spiritual Journey of Vietnam Vets* (New York: Ballantine Books, 1986), 208; and Richard Schweitzer, *The Cross and the Trenches: Religious Faith and Doubt among British and American Great War Soldiers* (Westport, CT: Praeger, 2003), 20. For relevant biblical passages, see, for example, Matthew 5:43-44 and I John 4:7-10. Martin Luther, however, declared it an act of love to try to defeat the enemy as quickly and completely as possible in order to restore justice and show him mercy as quickly as possible. See his *Secular Authority: To What Extent It Should Be Obeyed* (1523), part iii.

43. Remarque, *All Quiet on the Western Front*, 272. Also see Joel Turnipseed, *Baghdad Express: A Gulf War Memoir* (New York: Penguin Books, 2003), 79; and Bruce Norton, *Force Recon Diary, 1969* (New York: Ivy Books, 1991), 250-1. The allusion is to Shakespeare's famous lines in *Henry V*: "We few, we happy few, we band of brothers/ For he today that sheds his blood with me/ Shall be my brother" (scene iv, act III, line 60). Quotation taken from Justin Kaplan, ed., *Bartlett's Familiar Quotations* (Boston: Little, Brown and Co., 1992 [16th ed.]), 185.

44. Hardwick, *Down South*, ix; Hampton, 143; Cash, *A Table in the Presence*, 219; *Hearts and Minds*, Criterion Collection (2002); and John McCain, *Faith of My Fathers* (New York: Random House, 1999), 257.

45. A German at Stalingrad wrote in a letter: "But faith—faith in a good cause—is dead, as dead as I, together with a hundred thousand others, will be a month from now." In *Last Letters from Stalingrad*, 116.

46. Klemperer, *I Will Bear Witness*, 472.

47. Sam Watkins, *Co. Aytch: A Confederate Memoir of the Civil War* (New York: Touchstone, 2003), 150.

48. See James Hillman, *A Terrible Love of War* (New York: Penguin Press, 2004), 178-9.

Chapter Four

Is War Hell?

To me it was manifestly senseless to link a God of Love in any way with the kind of calculated murder I had been engaged in. How could one invite any member of the Trinity ... to pay heed and co-operate as one was coolly preparing to shatter the lovely red scalp of a German officer?
—J.R. Bellerby, British Army, First World War

He tried to summon up that American-fighting-man resolve, the will to live that even then was keeping hundreds of POW's alive all over Southeast Asia in even worse conditions. Maverick felt none of it, no indomitable courage, no esprit, no defiance, and sure as s—t no belief in God. He took no refuge in religion, organized or otherwise. He was absolutely certain that if there were a God, he would have gotten him out of the cage long ago. If there were a God, Ty wouldn't be dead; in fact, if there were a God, none of this s—t would even be happening and everbody'd be home in the U.S. of A. with his wife and babies
—Denis J. Marvicsin, Cobra pilot, Vietnam

Chaplains can say that God is present for men in war or that God presides sovereignly over all things. Chaplains can seek to rouse troops with unwelcome sermons about God's assistance to combatants.[1] But chaplains cannot change what war is. And they, too, can see war's sometimes vivid senselessness. Russell Stroup, serving in the Pacific in 1944, was continually conscious of the care of providence and he hoped that God would bless the efforts of U.S. troops against tyranny, but he could also see war as a realm of madness and futility.[2]

Chaplains can do good works—attempting to raise the morale of the hospitalized; praying with the wounded before surgery; helping to stop the spread of disease; baptizing battlefield converts; giving away New Testaments; trying to stem the corruption of combatants' souls; insisting that places of worship be built in war zones; relaying messages from loved ones; counseling the psychologically disturbed and men whose wives have had affairs; and arranging for

---

1. Sam Watkins, *Co. Aytch: A Confederate Memoir of the Civil War* (New York: Touchstone, 2003), 87. In *Jarhead: A Marine's Chronicle of the Gulf War and Other Battles* (New York: Pocket Books, 2003), Anthony Swofford writes: "[W]hen we get hit, there won't be a priest within miles" (237).
2. Russell Cartwright Stroup, *Letters from the Pacific: A Combat Chaplain in World War II*, ed., Richard Cartwright Austin (Columbia: University of Missouri Press, 2000), 24 and 41-3.

military personnel to go home in case of family emergencies.[3] But combat chaplains themselves can feel helpless, depressed, enraged, and spiritually wounded.[4] And in the context of war, good deeds can seem irrelevant. "Today at the orphanage, the chaplain and the Red Cross volunteers were playing the guitar and singing hymns like 'Jesus Loves Me' in Vietnamese," wrote a combat surgeon. "It was very touching. Indeed, it was almost overwhelming; I soon had to get out of the place," he continued, "and *back to reality*"—to a reality where, for most Christians, Jesus' involvement is hardly imaginable—to a reality of hell on earth.[5]

As with religious references in war memoirs generally, the description of combat and its consequences as "hell" is metaphorical. Consider the leaflets dropped on villages in Vietnam depicting weapons with torturous teeth and claws of wild animals besetting people "in the manner of the fantastic devils in medieval paintings of Hell."[6] Or consider the recollection that, in battle, machine guns rattle like demons, and the actions of the diabolical enemy evoke memories of childhood lessons about the terrors of hell.[7] The ubiquity of this language forces one to consider whether it points to something actual.

Memoirists say that, when the shooting starts, all hell breaks loose, and civilians caught between the battling sides "catch hell."[8] A year in Vietnam seemed like a personal "tour in hell," and a chaplain wondered if God let him taste that "wet hell" to help him experience what combatants felt.[9] Soldiers in Vietnam sported patches that said "I spent my time in hell."[10] A Marine in the Second World War thought that the Japanese were "mean as hell" and that his leading American officers were "crazy as hell."[11] A Civil War soldier with the 54th Massachusetts wrote about how what he experienced brought to mind "the

3. Bob Stoffey, *Cleared Hot! The Diary of a Marine Combat Pilot in Vietnam* (New York: St. Martin's 1992), 45, 62-3, 66-8; Byron E. Holley, *Vietnam, 1968-1969: A Battalion Surgeon's Journal* (New York: Ivy Books, 1993), 70; Stroup, *Letters from the Pacific*, 17, 53, 98, 137; James Johnson, *Combat Chaplain: A Thirty-Year Vietnam Battle* (Denton, TX: University of North Texas Press, 2001), 18, 52, 60-1, 107, 122, 190, 217 and 220. For many brief accounts of chaplains' service, see Thomas R. O'Brien, *Blessings from the Battlefield* (Huntington, IN: Our Sunday Visitor Publishing, 2002).
4. Johnson, *Combat Chaplain*, 133, 143, 155, 184, 206, and 221-223.
5. Holley, *Vietnam*, 58 and 190. Italics in the original.
6. Jonathan Schell, *The Real War: The Classic Reporting on the Vietnam War* (New York: Pantheon, 1987), 72.
7. E.B. Sledge, *With the Old Breed: At Peleliu and Okinawa* (New York: Oxford University Press, 1981), 65; and Earl Schenck Miers, ed., *When the World Ended: The Diary of Emma LeConte* (Lincoln: University of Nebraska Press, 1987), 49 and 51.
8. Holley, *Vietnam*, 35; Wallace Terry, *Bloods: An Oral History of the Vietnam War by Black Veterans* (New York: Ballantine Books, 1984), 25.
9. Johnson, *Combat Chaplain*, 1, 16, 37, 41, 59 and 78.
10. John L. Rotundo and Don Ericson, *Charlie Rangers* (New York: Ivy Books, 1989), 3.
11. Sledge, *With the Old Breed*, 150.

place prepared for the ungodly."[12] The words Sam Watkins used to describe Civil War combat with the First Tennessee Regiment are stark:

> The very air seemed full of stifling smoke and fire which seemed the very pit of hell, peopled by contending demons.... It seemed that the hot flames of hell were turned loose in all their fury, while the demons of damnation were hissing and laughing in flames, like seething serpents hissing out their rage.... The death-angel shrieks and laughs and old Father Time is busy with his sickle, as he gathers in the last harvest of death.... [I]n fifty yards of where I was the scene was lit up by fires that seemed like hell itself.[13]

To be in war is to be "scared as hell."[14] The lucky guys with million-dollar wounds—injuries serious enough to get them out of combat but not debilitating in the long-term—are said to be "on their way out of hell."[15] A combat chaplain in the Pacific criticized evangelists who wanted to scare soldiers into conversion with the threat of hell. Soldiers were not afraid of hell, the chaplain said; they had already lived in its borderland.[16] "Clearly I've never been there," said a journalist in Baghdad at the beginning of the Gulf War in 1991, "but this feels like we're in the center of hell."[17] Long after some combat veterans have returned home, they still find themselves locked in a "personal hell."[18]

Christians have different views on what hell is. It is a location or a state of being; it is a site of endless torment, an abyss of smoke and flame, a blazing inferno; or it is "the ultimate big stick to threaten people with." Hell is a place of deep, everlasting misery where people are irreparably cut off from the presence of God and the possibility of peace. Hell is termination, annihilation, the place where "being fades away into non-entity;"[19] it is "God's withdrawal from the

---

12. Virginia M. Adams, ed., *On the Altar of Freedom: A Black Soldier's Civil War Letters from the Front* (New York: Warner Books, 1991), 26.

13. Watkins, *Co. Aytch*, 48, 169, 220.

14. George Wilson, *If You Survive* (New York: Ballantine Books, 1987), 117.

15. Sledge, *With the Old Breed*, 130; and Wilson, *If You Survive*, 145.

16. Stroup, *Letters from the Pacific*, 134.

17. Bernard Shaw, recorded in *Desert Storm: The War Begins*, VHS, directed by Bernard Shaw (Universal City, CA: Turner Home Entertainment, 1991). After further reflection, Shaw emphasized and expanded on this point. See the beginning of *Desert Storm: The Victory*, VHS, directed by Bernard Shaw (Universal City, CA: Turner Home Entertainment, 1991). And so on: "This war would be hell if they weren't even shooting.... You know what? War *really* is Hell." See Lynn Hampton, *The Fighting Strength: Memoirs of a Combat Nurse in Vietnam* (New York: Warner Books, 1990), 65 and 43; and Edwin Campion Vaughn, *Some Desperate Glory: The World War I Diary of a British Officer, 1917* (New York: Henry Holt and Company, 1981), 196.

18. William P. Mahedy, *Out of the Night: The Spiritual Journey of Vietnam Vets* (New York: Ballantine Books, 1986), 4.

19. William Crockett, ed., *Four Views on Hell* (Grand Rapids: Zondervan Publishing House, 1992), 29, 31, 37, 39, 57, 62, 76, 137. For a brief discussion of the concept of hell in Christian tradition, see the entry for hell in Adrian Hastings, *Oxford Companion to*

human soul," the "ultimate darkness of body and soul," an "unabated sadness because of what is yearned for, but always lacking."[20] Hell is separation from God; the abode of torment for the unrepentant. Hell's exactions are physical, mental, and spiritual. Hell is the privation of everything heavenly and the fulfillment and definitive contentedness that the kingdom of heaven symbolizes. Hell is the consequence people pay for poor decisions and wayward actions. Whether hell is construed as a horrific abode of fire-and-brimstone or as a merely unpleasant underworld—whether hell is eternal or temporary—no one, after experiencing it, would want to stay there or return to it.[21]

Early Christian visions of hell likened it to a site of human sacrifice, a place of great darkness and lostness. Some Christians have envisioned devils seeking to bring as many people to hell as possible. The Church father Tertullian described hell as "that great vault of eternal fire" and as a "the pool of fire." Augustine suggested that nature's laws were suspended in hell, where people endure mental torture but never go insane, and burn forever but are never consumed. Luther construed hell as a great nothingness; Jonathan Edwards described it as the place where "God's saving grace, mercy and pity are gone forever, never for a moment to return." [22]

Each of these descriptions of hell—comprising physical and spiritual termination, fire, misery, the feeling of endlessness, loss, and loneliness—resonates (in one way or another) with the experience of combat. So, too, does the one thing the descriptions have in common: the feeling that, in combat, God is not there. "Where was God when we went through hell in Vietnam?" a veteran asks. The response: "He was smart, he went AWOL."[23] Perhaps this is because war is about death and, in the words of one Catholic theologian, death is an "expression of the realm of Satan as ruler of this world."[24]

Christian Thought (Oxford: Oxford University Press, 2000). For an overview of the treatment of the concept in literature, see the entry for hell in David Lyle Jeffrey, *A Dictionary of Biblical Tradition in English Literature* (Grand Rapids: Eerdmans, 1992).

20. Email messages to author from, in order of quotation, from theologians Galen Johnson (August 13, 2006), Robbie Castleman (August 14, 2006), and Breck Castleman (August 16, 2006).

21. Chuck Crisafulli and Kyra Thompson, *Go to Hell* (New York: Simon Spotlight Entertainment, 2005), 7.

22. Tertullian, *Treatises on Penance: On Penitence and on Purity* trans. William Saint (New York: Newman Press, 1959), 11 and 35; Richard Marius, *Martin Luther: The Christian between God and Death* (Cambridge, MA: Belknap Press of Harvard University Press, 1999), 60-3; Clark H. Pinnock, "The Destruction of the Finally Impenitent" *Criswell Theological Review* 4 (Spring 1990): 243-59; and Robert A. Peterson, "The Dark Side of Eternity: Hell as Eternal Conscious Punishment" *Christian Research Journal* 30.4 (2007), 13-21.

23. Uwe Siemon-Netto, *The Acquittal of God: A Theology for Vietnam Veterans* (New York: Pilgrim Press, 1990), 13.

24. Karl Rahner, *On the Theology of Death* (New York: Herder and Herder, 1969), 51.

Or, even if God is there in the combat zone, battle does not afford one the opportunity to think about it. At the least, in the context of battle God is hidden and, it seems, temporarily irrelevant.[25]

And, so far as Christian veterans say, Jesus' involvement in combat is impossible to imagine. What, the researcher asks, would Jesus have done if he were present at a battle with the Nazis? The interviewee is perplexed: "Jesus doesn't try to destroy anything," he says. "He was a loving man....He wants to draw people to himself."[26]

What would Jesus have done if he were at the battle of Peleliu?
"He would put out his hands, say 'peace,' and the fighting would stop."[27]

What if Jesus were at the battle for Okinawa?
"He would have shared the Gospel with everyone—Japanese and American—and if everyone accepted it, the war would be unnecessary."

"He would make it stop. He'd say 'Be still' and the artillery wouldn't work any longer." [28]

If Jesus could speak with the crew of a B-24 on a bombing mission over Germany, what would he say?
"He'd say, 'I hate war; I don't like war.'"[29]

These quotes come from Christian combat veterans of the Second World War. They believed, and still believe (rationally), that the wars against Japan and the Nazis were necessary.

Necessary, they say—yet they also say that it is impossible to see Jesus in the context of combat. Defeating the Nazis meant firing artillery, and defeating the Nazis was a good thing—yet they cannot see Jesus firing the artillery. Ending Japanese atrocities against civilians in Asia involved the use of flamethrowers, and ending Japanese atrocities was a good thing—but they cannot see Jesus operating the flamethrower.

---

25. For commentary on this theme, see Mister Thorne, "Atheists in Foxholes, Christians in Uniforms," *Humanist* 63:3 (2003), 19-23.
26. Second World War veteran in discussion with Preston Jones, Siloam Springs, Arkansas, May 30, 2006.
27. Second World War veteran in discussion with Preston Jones, John Brown University, June 29, 2006.
28. Second World War veterans in discussion with Preston Jones, John Brown University, June 6, 2006.
29. Second World War veteran in discussion with Preston Jones, Siloam Springs, Arkansas, June 28, 2006.

The theme holds for other conflicts.

What would Jesus do if he met a platoon on patrol in a Vietnamese jungle?
"He would be disappointed…. His message would be communicated more through a look than through words—a look of disappointment."[30]

Where would Jesus fit in the context of a combat mission in Vietnam?
"He would have figured out another way."[31]

What if Jesus were in Saigon during the Tet Offensive?
"He wouldn't have been there. He would have found another way…. He would have helped his people to protect themselves and get out of there."[32]

If a skirmish against the Taliban broke out and Jesus was there, what would he do?
"He would have tried to calm the conflict…. He may have gotten killed but he wouldn't have killed…. He wouldn't have fought back…. He would have preached to both sides."[33]

What would Jesus do in southern Afghanistan?
"He would wait for a time when the Taliban were unarmed, and he'd talk with them."[34]

It is the warrior's inability to see Jesus in the context of battle that makes the work of Christian chaplains problematic.[35] Chaplains administer Holy Communion to Marines who have come to doubt God's presence or who have fallen away from their faith,[36] but the chaplains' own petitions seem weak next to the unplanned semi-conscious and quickly forgotten prayers wrenched from warriors at a battle's start.[37] Chaplains pray for the protection and survival of

---

30. Vietnam veteran in discussion with Preston Jones, John Brown University, June 9, 2006.
31. Vietnam Veteran, discussion with Preston Jones, Eagle River, Alaska, July 27, 2006.
32. Vietnam veteran, telephone discussion with Preston Jones, May 24, 2006.
33. Afghanistan conflict veteran, discussion with Preston Jones, Siloam Springs, Arkansas, May 30, 2006.
34. Afghanistan conflict veteran, discussion with Preston Jones, Eagle River, Alaska, July 15, 2006.
35. Mahedy, *Out of the Night*, discusses the "bitterness" some combat veterans feel toward chaplains (133).
36. See, for example, Sledge, *With the Old Breed*, 242; and see *Platoon*, MGM Home Entertainment (2001), in which one soldier says: "A Christian don't go around a village cuttin' off heads and shit."
37. Ches Schneider, *Classrooms to Claymores: A Teacher at War in Vietnam* (New York: Ivy Books, 1999), 165.

troops on their side, but this necessarily involves the elimination or incapacita-
tion of people on the other side.[38] That is how war is; but the Christian fighter
cannot visualize Jesus in it.

So, for Christian warriors, combat means, in some way, putting Jesus aside.
It means putting one's soul in a lost-and-found department for a while—it means
feeling like one is trapped in a bottomless pit.[39] It means that the combatant's
personal theological reflections must focus on the warfare of the Hebrew Bible
or, to a lesser extent, the violence in the book of Revelation.[40] Sometimes warriors consciously pass Jesus over in favor of the "Old Testament God—the tough,
harsh, severe, vengeful, eye-for-an-eye desert deity."[41] The deity of war is the
"Great Giver of victory," the "God of battles," not the prophet who washed his
disciples' feet.[42] Sometimes warriors see themselves as almost becoming godlike as they mete retribution to the hard-hearted.[43]

Or warfare means that the combatant must embrace civil religion, constru-
ing Jesus as a sort of rifle-toting John Wayne.[44] "God ordains and chooses the
government and the military for a high and noble purpose," Chaplain Cash tells
us. "And the man who chooses to enter its ranks, whether he knows it or not, is
serving more than his country; he's serving God."[45] But combatants say that
they wonder what war is doing to their souls,[46] and some of them mimic the

---

38. See Joel Turnipseed, *Baghdad Express: A Gulf War Memoir* (New York: Penguin
Books, 2003), 81. At the beginning of documentary *The Anderson Platoon*, VHS, directed by Pierre Schoendoerffer (Homevision, 2000), a Catholic chaplain prays: "Deign
O Lord to rescue me. Let all be put to shame and confusion who seek to snatch away my
life. Deign O Lord to rescue me. Amen." See Psalm 40:13-14. Pope John Paul II wrote
that faith in the Virgin Mary's protection had at one point helped the Poles to conquer an
invader but, here again, there is no sense that Mary might also be interested in the lives of
the men comprising the invader's army. See John Paul II, *Rise, Let Us Be on Our Way*
(New York: Warner Books, 2004), 52.
39. Johnson, *Combat Chaplain*, 2 and 12.
40. Of the 51 biblical references in the war memoir of Chaplain Carey Cash, 35 cite or
refer to Old Testament scriptures. See Cash, *A Table in the Presence: The Dramatic Account of How a U.S. Marine Battalion Experienced God's Presence amidst the Chaos of
the War in Iraq* (Nashville: W Publishing Group, 2004). Also see Hampton, *Fighting
Strength*, 219; and Denis Marvicsin, *Maverick: The Personal War of a Vietnam Cobra
Pilot*. New York: Jove Books, 1996), 60. And see John Ketwig, ... *and a Hard Rain Fell:
A GI's True Story of the War in Vietnam* (Naperville, IL: Sourcebooks, 2002), where he
wonders if combat helicopters were predicted in the book of Revelation (259).
41. Richard Marcinko, *Rogue Warrior* (New York: Pocket Star Books, 1992), 108.
42. Gooding, *On the Altar of Freedom*, 85; Emil Rosenblatt and Ruth Rosenblatt, *Hard
Marching Every Day: The Civil War Letters of Private Wilbur Fisk, 1861-1865* (Lawrence: University Press of Kansas, 1983), 321.
43. Mahedy, *Out of the Night*, 16.
44. Ibid., 141-2.
45. Here in *Table in the Presence*, 209, Cash is quoting a Vietnam veteran.
46. See Philipp Witkop, *German Students' War Letters* trans. A. F. Wedd (Philadelphia:
Pine Street Books, 2002): "What is the good of escaping all the bullets and shells, if my

Scriptures: "Yea tho I walk thru the Valley of the Shadow of Death, I will fear no Evil, 'cause I am the Meanest SOB in the Valley!"[47]

Chaplain Cash's claim is nonsense: with very few exceptions, Christian combat veterans in the twentieth century do not say that they fought for God;[48] even some veterans of the Civil War were skeptical of preachers who claimed God's favor for their cause.[49] Some chaplains involved in different wars denied that soldiers, after experiencing combat, were motivated by patriotism—for soldiers fight to survive; they fight for their buddies; they fight because they want to make it home.[50] "I believe I will be much closer to God here than when I arrived," a soldier in Vietnam wrote to his wife, only soon to conclude that war places one's conscience in a no-win situation. "The only major objective we each have is to stay alive another day," he wrote, "and if innocent farmers get killed along the way, it's better them than us."[51]

Non-combatant chaplains can consecrate battle, assuring soldiers of the glory of sacrifice for country,[52] promoting Jesus as a cold warrior or as a despiser of conscientious objectors. They can preach about a Jesus in khaki and

---

soul is injured?" (21). Also see Tim O'Brien, *If I Die in a Combat Zone, Box Me Up and Ship Me Home* (New York: Dell Publishing, 1973), 66; and Johnson, *Combat Chaplain*, 4 and 55. And see Mahedy, *Out of the Night*, 6.

47. Holley, *Vietnam,* 115. A variation is: "Yea, if I must walk through the valley, let me take the gunny [sergeant] with me." Also see William H. Hardwick, *Down South: One Tour in Vietnam* (New York: Ballantine Books, 2004), xiv; Ketwig, ... *and a Hard Rain Fell*, 79-80; and Bruce H. Norton, *Force Recon Diary, 1969* (New York: Ivy Books, 1991), 62.

48. When this monograph was near completion a retired army chaplain read it. In an email to Jones, the chaplain wrote: "I started reading [Chaplain] Cash's book while I was in Iraq. I was impressed, but could only read about 40% before I just put it away. It was nothing like my experience or the experiences of my four Chaplains, two of which had route clearance engineer battalions and two who had infrastructure building engineer battalions."

49. O'Brien, *If I Die in a Combat Zone*, recalls an otherwise belligerent chaplain saying: "Of course Vietnam is no crusade for Christ.... [M]aybe no war is really fought for God." (65). And see William A. Fletcher, *Rebel Private: Front and Rear* (New York: Meridian, 1997), 2-3, 153.

50. Stroup, *Letters from the Pacific*, 157-8; and Johnson, *Combat Chaplain*, 3. Memoirs and diaries of the Second World War, and interviews with combatants of that war, do not bear out the claim, made in 1945, that finding "heaven in a foxhole" was a "typical" experience among combatants. See Clyde H. Denis, ed., *These Live On: The Best of True Stories Unveiling the Power and Presence of God in World War II* (Chicago: Good Books, 1945), 1, 3-5.

51. Holley, *Vietnam*, 29 and 48.

52. O'Brien, *If I Die in a Combat* Zone, 62-65; Erich Maria Remarque, *All Quiet on the Western Front* (New York: Random House, 1982), 204. This point was driven home to Jones (author) after he heard a non-combatant army chaplain speak on the high calling of being prepared to die for one's country. The day before the sermon, a combat veteran who had been in firefights in Iraq (2003) told Jones that he did not think God had anything to do with war.

imagine him firing machine guns. They can sound like other officers who sur-mise that "even God wants the Marines to go kick some Iraqi ass."[53] But warri-ors themselves see the inadequacy of this. They know there is little comfort to be found in the insincere rationalization that the death of a friend in combat is a good thing since God must have willed it,[54] or in the serene visage of a statue of the Virgin Mary presiding over a hopelessly overcrowded war zone orphanage. Combatants can see the godlessness of war in a crucifix blasted to pieces by artillery, and by churches bombed out or appropriated for the purposes of war—as resting places, observation posts, and snipers' nests.[55] A Catholic infantry

---

53. On dressing Jesus in khaki, see James A. Hillman, *A Terrible Love of War* (New York: Penguin Press, 2004), 185. On the officer's words, see Turnipseed, *Baghdad Express*, 7. One the remaining points, see Ben Sherman, *Medic! The Story of a Conscientious Objector in the Vietnam War* (New York: Writer's Club Press, 2002), 159. Michael Herr, *Dispatches* (New York: Vintage International, 1977), recalls: "Sermonettes came over Armed Forces radio every couple of hours, once I heard a chaplain from the 9th Division starting up, 'Oh gawd, help us to learn to live with Thee in a more dynamic way in these perilous times, that we may better serve Thee in this struggle against Thine enemies....'" (45). Theological reflection on combat does not come naturally to many veterans. Of 70 interview manuscripts from WWII veterans reviewed at the National Museum of the Pacific War, just 8 included voluntary theological reflection, primarily in brief asides or as parenthetical clauses. Among these transcripts theological reflection pervades only the spoken memoirs of Thomas Bousman, a child of missionaries in the Philippines at the time of Second World War. He and his family were interned, though not tortured, by the Japanese. Other files that include some theological content are: R. Murphy Williams, Glen McDole, Jay Bollmen, Helen Beattie, Kyle Thompson, Elliott Ross, and Lawrence Norris.

54. James R. McDonough, *Platoon Leader: A Memoir of Command in Combat* (New York: Ballantine, 1985), 190. McDonough writes: "Although Wilson did not appear to be an overly religious man, I sensed that the only way to console him was to explain the death as God's will. Personally, I could see no point in that proposition. Evans's death had served no purpose; as far as I could tell, it had been a blunder.... Although I couldn't follow the logic of my own words, they seemed to lighten Wilson's load .... [T]ogether we groped for meaning in a man's death. I did my best to conceal my own skepticism.... Somehow we came to the conclusion that Evans's death was a good thing: it must be good if God willed it."

55. Vaughn, *Some Desperate Glory*, 15-16, 18, 89, 107, 155. Also see Hampton, *Fighting Strength*, 50; Jonathan Schell, *The Real War: The Classic Reporting on the Vietnam War* (New York: Pantheon Books, 1987), 320, 322 and 350; Wilson, *If You Survive*, 253-4; Marvicsin, *Maverick*, 118; Johnson, *Combat Chaplain*, 188 and 194; and Siegfried Knappe and Ted Brusaw, *Soldat: Reflections of a German Soldier, 1936-1949* (New York: Dell Publishing, 1992), 128, 280 and 320. In *Saving Private Ryan,* DVD, directed by Steven Spielberg (Burbank, CA: Dreamworks Home Entertainment, 1999) soldiers discuss the rigors of war while resting in an abandoned French church. Later a sniper takes up a position in a church tower. Schweitzer recounts the experience of one WWI soldier who refused to participate in the artillery shelling of a church. See Richard Schweitzer, *The Cross and the Trenches: Religious Faith and Doubt among British and American Great War Soldiers* (Westport, CT: Praeger, 2003), 207.

officer in the First World War wondered at the presence of his men in a place "where gentle nuns and children had so often knelt at benediction."[56]

War is a spiritual abyss, an empire of spiritual devastation.[57] The rational, loving God of Sunday school and seminary does not fit.[58] War makes it seem that there is something terribly wrong with the God of the warrior's childhood.[59] One veteran wrote that he and most of those he served with had been raised with a "central godly ethic," but they learned that such a thing was out of place in a combat zone.[60] Some young warriors who start out pursuing godliness give it up after experiencing combat.[61] They wonder why it is alright to kill other men but a sin to visit prostitutes.[62]

Before battle, one combatant prayed to say goodbye to God until the violence was over. "I told God I was about to take leave of my faith for a few days."[63] A survivor of the Battle of the Somme recalled that from the day the battle began all his religion died. "All my teaching and beliefs in God had left me, never to return."[64] Vera Brittain, a nurse in Malta and France during the First World War, wrote that her belief in the efficacy of prayer died with the men she loved and cared for.[65]

And, as we have seen, the wartime military provides an alternative kind of faith, along with respite from parental piety and relief from the feeling that life must make sense.[66] A regular churchgoer before and during war contemplated

---

56. Vaughn, *Some Desperate Glory*, 184.

57. Stroup, *Letters from the Pacific*, 43.

58. Schweitzer, *Cross and the Trenches*, 68.

59. Siemon-Netto, *Acquittal of God*, 41. Mahedy, *Out of the Night*, writes: "A great many Vietnam veterans have become religious agnostics or are now hostile to religion because they took seriously what they learned in Bible classes or in the parochial schools about killing.... Not only was the American religious experience but authentic biblical faith was called into serious question" (31-2).

60. McDonough, *Platoon Leader*, 77.

61. An interviewee in *Winter Soldier*, DVD, directed by Winterfilm Collective (New York: New Yorker Video, 1972) tells of a highly religious Mormon who, as time went, put godliness aside. Also see Turnipseed, *Baghdad Express*, 181.

62. Mahedy, *Out of the Night*, 7.

63. Andrew Exum, *This Man's Army: A Soldier's Story from the Front Lines of the War on Terrorism* (New York: Gotham, 2005), xii and 177. Exum writes: "My Presbyterian guilt doesn't allow me to consider that I somehow won't be held responsible for what I have done when I stand before the Almighty one day" (177).

64. Sgt. C. Bartram quoted in Martin Middlebrook, *The First Day on the Somme, 1 July 1916* (New York: Penguin Books, 1971), 316.

65. Vera Brittain, *Testament of Youth: An Autobiographical Study of the Years, 1900-1925* (New York: Penguin Books, 1978), 23.

66. Swofford, *Jarhead*, 155.

the "mad fate" that drags men into war.[67] Another soldier prayed but still felt hopeless. Some lose faith even in a mother's prayers.[68]

Most combatants continue to believe that God exists in the same way that they believe the planet Mercury exists—it is a cold fact. But many come to doubt that God can be trusted, at least in the world of war. They do not arrive at unbelief in an atheistic sense but, to use Paul Tillich's phrase, many do come to a place of "un-faith." In their youth, America's young men learned about a faithful God who watches out for them and who will not let them down, who will let them triumph over evil and preserve them in adversity. But in war, things often do not turn out this way.[69]

Combatants and war veterans handle the cognitive dissonance they feel by theologically bracketing their war experiences and placing them in a unique mental universe. Otherwise articulate Christian war veterans have trouble speaking about war in theologically coherent ways—in ways that move past easy and usually evasive phrases—"God is in the control," "it's all a mystery," and so on.[70]

The hellishness of war presses from all sides. In a battle zone it is impossible to see the enemy as people made in the image of God; they are more like dead animals on the side of the road.[71] "I never saw people," a former sniper told a class of Christian university students. "I saw targets. If you see people, you hesitate, and you get killed."[72]

War is merciless—it makes you indifferent to the cries of strangers. In a war zone you hate or you struggle against hate.[73] War is "mud, booby traps, bullets, ambushes, walking point, no sleep, [and being] scared stiff with each slight sound."[74] In war, putting the fear of God into an enemy is to devastate him, dismember him, or to be indifferent to him.[75] Battle is the inglorious death of a

---

67. Vaughn, *Some Desperate Glory*, 48. Also Johnson, *Combat Chaplain*, writes: "morality has a way of becoming blurred in our quest to survive" (135).
68. Sledge, *With the Old Breed*, 63; Remarque, *All Quiet on the Western Front*, 183.
69. See Siemon-Netto, *Acquittal of God*, 40-1.
70. This statement is based on the authors' many conversations with Christian war veterans. Also see Cash's, *Table in the Presence*, a veritable compendium of evangelical clichés.
71. See Philip Caputo, *A Rumor of War* (New York: Henry Holt, 1977), 179. In a discussion with Preston Jones, a former sniper used this common metaphor when talking about dead Vietcong. And see, Knappe, *Soldat*, 53-54. It is striking that in his *Table in the Presence*, Chaplain Cash never grants humanity to the enemy.
72 Vietnam veteran (sniper), interviewed by Preston Jones, John Brown University, October 2006.
73. Caputo, *Rumor of War*, xix and 110; and Stroup, *Letters from the Pacific*, 19. In *Faith of My Fathers*, John McCain writes that hate "sustains the fighter in his devotion to the complete destruction of his enemy and helps to overcome the virtuous human impulse to recoil in disgust from what must be done by your hand" (76).
74. Johnson, *Combat Chaplain*, 124.
75. Caputo, *Rumor of War*, 77.

buddy who had volunteered to fill your canteen at a muddy river only to be taken down by a sniper.[76] War is the euphemization of legs blown off by mines as "traumatic amputation."[77] War is trophy collecting—enemy helmets, flags, rifles, ears, gold teeth, skulls, complete bodies (for photographs), identification cards, and Bibles.[78] Combat is feeling as if God is playing a trick on you; it is the recognition that evil resides in ordinary people;[79] it is feeling sorry for animals but not for the people caught in a crossfire.[80]

War is wandering in a spiritual wilderness. An unarmed medic in beautiful Vietnam wondered how God could ignore so much human agony while maintaining the wonders of the natural world.[81] A chaplain in Desert Storm called war darkness, horror, and a "cancerous crud." A crazed field morgue worker declared, "Ain't no Jesus in Vietnam!"[82] And a surgeon confessed to finding no solace in prayer and Bible reading.[83] A chaplain wrote that it was difficult to discern when or how God's intervention came to god-forsaken Vietnam.[84]

Warriors sense that God is disinterested in battle, that he does not have anything to do with it.[85] If he does—if he chooses who lives and dies—if he could stop war and does not—what kind of God does that make him?

Veterans remind us that the conditions war creates can bring out the best in people: heroism, selflessness, compassion, tolerance, and forgiveness. Veterans tell us that war drags a person into the abyss and yet provides thorough "training

---

76. Cherokee Paul McDonald, *Into the Green: A Reconnaissance by Fire* (New York: Plume Book, 2001), 161.

77. Caputo, *Rumor of War*, , 167.

78. Sledge, *With the Old Breed*, xiii and 118, Caputo, *Rumor of War,* 67; Tim O'Brien, *If I Die in a Combat Zone,* 87; Hampton, *Fighting Strength*, 71; Sherman, *Medic!*, 208; Stoup, *Letters from the Pacific*, 45 and 54; Terry, *Bloods*, 24; and Johnson, *Combat Chaplain*, 56 and 118; Robert Hunt Rhodes, ed., *All for the Union: The Civil War Diary and Letters of Elisha Hunt Rhodes* (New York: Orion Books, 1985), 25. In an interview with Preston Jones, one veteran of Operation Iraqi Freedom displayed an identity card taken from a dead Iraqi soldier.

79. Caputo, *Rumor of War*, 231, 331.

80. Herr, *Dispatches*, 28. Sympathy for animals alongside a loss of sympathy for people is a surprisingly common theme in combat memoirs. See, for example, Hampton, *Fighting Strength*, 209; Remarque, *All Quiet on the Western Front*, 62; Schell, *Real War,* 131; and Robert Mason, *Chickenhawk: A Shattering Personal Account of the Helicopter War in Vietnam* (New York: Penguin, 1984), 340.

81. Sherman, *Medic!*, 139. Also see Stroup, *Letters from the Pacific*, 41; and Marvicsin, *Maverick*, 216.

82. John Sack, *Company C: The Real War in Iraq* (New York: Avon Books, 1995), 209; Sherman, *Medic!*, 60. The black morgue attendant went on to say: "Jesus a black man. Desert niggah. Come outta the Holy Land. Moses too. Desert Niggahs, all of 'em" (61).

83. Holley, *Vietnam*, 162.

84. Johnson, *Combat Chaplain*, 125.

85. See Swofford, *Jarhead*, 319.

for the human soul."[86] But reflection on the good things of battle comes in response to war's fundamental tragedies.[87] Combat memoirs do not focus on good times. And if God is good, then where in war is he? A wounded man put this question to a nurse but she did not know; she, too, had come to doubt that God cared.[88] "It is easy to believe God is involved and cares when life is easy," says a child of missionaries, a Christian veteran of the invasion of Iraq in 2003,

> but to believe that God is involved on a daily level in Iraq would mean God has a hand in the events there and that doesn't match up with what a [benevolent] higher being would do. Seeing kids die did it for me. They had nothing to do with the war and never had a chance. It is hard to believe a fair and just God could have a hand in a 5-year-old girl getting run over by a truck while trying to beg for food, or [in the experience of] a little boy with no legs and one arm because his house got hit by a tank round [which] killed both his parents but left him crippled.[89]

Concepts of hell in Christian traditions differ, but what they have in common is the sense that hell exists apart from God's presence. Wherever God is not, that is hell. And whatever hell is, the words combatants use to describe war correspond, in general ways, to the Christian tradition's perceptions of it. War breeds cynicism, despair, madness, bitterness, horror, and a sense of doom.[90] War is brutish, primitive, savage, wild, inhumane, exhausting, excruciating, angry, frustrating, and self-defeating; it makes men filthy and haggard. In the words of a German soldier at Stalingrad, war breeds "[m]isery, hunger, cold, renunciation, doubt, despair and horrible death."[91] War evinces wild babbling, animalistic guttural noises, grunts, and hideous, agonized, and prolonged screams; it extracts brutish yelling, terror, and tension. The air of war is heavy

---

86. This is a theme in Hampton, *Fighting Strength*, preface, 72, 137, and 171; and Philipp Witkop, ed., *German Students' War Letters* (Philadelphia: Pine Street Books, 2002), 150. A Vietnam veteran interviewed in *Combat Film*, VHS, directed by Lawrence Ptkethly (South Burlington, VT: Annenberg/CPB Collection, 1994) says that he misses the good relations black and white combatants had during the conflict.

87. In a discussion with Preston Jones, a veteran said that in Vietnam there were good times and bad times. Jones asked if he could interview the veteran to discuss the good times. The veteran declined, knowing that it is not possible to talk about the Vietnam conflict without remembering the bad times. Speaking with Cody Beckman, a corpsman said that he could see both heaven and hell in battle. However, even the heaven he described was in things like sewing up a Vietnamese girl hit by shrapnel well enough that she would not have a scar.

88. Hampton, *Fighting Strength*, 42, 136, 193, and 211.

89. Iraqi Freedom veteran, email to Preston Jones, May 15, 2006.

90. Herr, *Dispatches*, 58, 102-103; and Marvicsin, *Maverick*, 87.

91. Franz Schneider and Charles Gullans, eds. and trans., *Last Letters from Stalingrad* (New York: The Hudson Review, Inc., 1961), 38.

with repulsive odors.[92] Bodies mangled in battle, blown to bits or burned beyond
recognition seem unsalvageable for the Day of Judgment.[93]

And if hell comes after moral condemnation, some veterans are familiar
with it already, for, being unable to forgive themselves, they feel that God could
never forgive them for what they have done, for what they were compelled to
do, in battle.[94] If war is not some part of hell, a veteran of the battle for Okinawa
asked rhetorically, what possibly could be?

In his last letter home a German soldier at Stalingrad wrote that he had been
religious before the Second World War but this had changed in light of God's
absence in battle. "I have searched for God in every crater, in every destroyed
house, on every corner, in every friend, in my fox hole, and in the sky," he wrote
to his father, a pastor. "God did not show Himself, even though my heart cried
for Him....No, Father, there is no God."[95]

A very different memoir, this one from Vietnam, draws on similar language. The writer could still hear the screams of a sniper victim who cried
through the night and died just before an evacuation helicopter's arrival. "I see
[his cries] as the screams of every man who ever screamed at whatever pain had
been visited on him and laid siege to his courage, his strength, his senses, his
faith," the veteran writes:

> It was the roar of a shearing wind, all the fingernails of every deformed and
> twisted demon who had ever tormented Christ raked again and again across the
> chalkboard of reason.... Where in the living *f—k* is my piece-of-s—t guardian
> angel? Who the hell gave *it* a day off? For that matter, where is my loving
> God? Been hearing all about you since I was a kid. This is the kind of s—t you
> let happen to all of us little children you love as your own son?[96]

Stunned by war's madness, one warrior joked that maybe God was drunk or
stoned.[97]

---

92. Sledge, *With the Old Breed*, 34, 55, 60, 85, 102, 106-7, 120 and 143; and Johnson,
Combat Chaplain, 216.
93. Caputo, *Rumor of War*, writes: "I could not believe those bloody messes would be
capable of resurrection on the Last Day" (128). Also see Remarque, *All Quiet on the
Western Front*, 139.
94. Siemon-Netto, *Acquittal of God*, 21 and 37. Siemon-Netto quotes a combat veteran
who says: "For twenty years I see in my dreams the face of the first Vietnamese I shot the
day I arrived over there. He was an eight-year-old boy. The kid was about to thrown a
hand grenade onto our vehicle" (27). A colleague relates the account of a good friend of
his, a veteran of the Korean conflict, who says that God cannot forgive him for what he
had to do in battle at close range. Also see Mahedy, *Out of the Night*, 12-13 and 188.
95. Schneider, *Last Letters from Stalingrad*, 65. Another soldier whose letter is in the
same volume wrote: "I don't believe in God any more, because he betrayed us." (60)
96. McDonald, *Into the Green*, 93-95. Expletives edited. Italics in the original.
97. In *Platoon*, MGM Home Entertainment (2001), one character says: "If there's a God
in heaven...he's drunk as a fucking monkey and smoking shit."

On the one hand, Christian veterans are reluctant to say that God is absent from combat zones; the doctrine of God's omniscience makes one hesitate to do so. But the number of combat veterans who could see God's action amidst combat—as opposed to within their own souls or in retrospect—approaches zero. In some real sense, God *is* absent from combat. And because God is absent from combat, war, in some way, is hell.[98]

---

98. At the end of his war diary, *Some Desperate Glory,* Vaughn writes "I sat on the floor and gazed into a black and empty future" (232). McDonald, *Into the Green*, writes that after combat "[y]ou know in your heart you will never be clean again." Also see Tim O'Brien, *If I Die in a Combat Zone*, 136.

Chapter Five

Yet God Is There:
Toward a Theology of Combat

If our Lord had not suffered on this earth on the cross, I would blaspheme God all day if I believed in God at all. I only believe in God in this war because I believe in Jesus Christ the Crucified.
—David Railton, British chaplain, First World War

At one end of the clearing, prayerful hands had fashioned a Holy Table of bamboo on which were placed a cross and a lamp. The cross was a simply carved piece of wood.... The cross pointed us to our heavenly Father and at the same time reached out its arms to include us all in an expression of the Love that will never go.
—Ernest Gordon, POW, Second World War

War is hell; God seems absent from it. If substantial theological reflection among warriors takes place, it is almost always *after* the guns have stopped—when combatants are wounded and unable to fight, when they have been made prisoners of war and are completely at the mercy of others, or when the warring has ended.[1] Sometimes fighters are able to make sense of what they experienced

---

1. In Philipp Witkop, ed., *German Students' War Letters* (Philadelphia: Pine Street Books, 2002), a soldier writes: "I am lying on the battle-field badly wounded.... Jesus is with me, so it is easy to die" (155). Unlike combat memoirs, theological reflection (to varying extents) is common in POW memoirs. See, for example, Ernest Gordon, *To End All Wars* (Grand Rapids: Zondervan, 2002); Eric Lomax, *The Railway Man* (New York: Ballantine Books, 1995); Jesse L Miller, *Prisoner of Hope* (Englewood, CO: Cadence International, 1989); Sidney Stewart, *Give Us This Day* (New York: Avon Books, 1990); Robinson Risner, *The Passing of the Night* (New York: Ballantine Books, 1973); and C. Hoyt Watson, *The Amazing Story of Sergeant Jacob DeShazer* (Winona Lake, IN: Light and Life Press, 1950). Also see the unpublished interview transcripts of Harold Bousman held by the Oral History Program at the National Museum of the Pacific War, POW file. Bousman, a civilian captured by the Japanese in the Philippines, recounts his father (a minister) telling his imprisoned congregation, "unless you can forgive [the Japanese soldier], then you better think twice before you come forward to receive the Holy Communion." The striking thing is that each of these theologically informed memoirs is related by a prisoner who endured torture or the real threat of torture. But not all POW memoirs convey theological reflection. Some prisoners were sustained by their hatred of the enemy—one theme of Gordon's *To End All Wars*. Also see the interview transcripts of John Bumgartner and J.S. Gray in the POW file at the Museum of the Pacific War.

after they have returned home. But this is not always so. For some, war continues to be theologically troubling long after the guns have become silent. Anger
at a God who seemed to go AWOL in combat can remain and lead to spiritual
indifference or bewilderment, or to an enduring feeling of divine betrayal.[2] One
veteran claimed to have read the Bible every year since his time in war; he was
"looking for the explanation," but he could never find it.[3]

Christian combat veterans cannot see Jesus as a combatant. So a syllogism
arises: Jesus would have stopped the fighting; the fighting did not stop; so he
must not have been there.

Yet the complication that must be taken seriously is that some combat veterans say that they *did* feel God's presence in wartime. A navy officer who
could see the face of a kamikaze pilot in the process of attacking a nearby ship
reports that he felt near to God. A helicopter pilot, an infantryman, and an intel-
ligence gatherer in Vietnam read the Bible and prayed with others and main-
tained their faith; soldiers in southern France and Belgium in 1944 sensed that
God was with them; and an Air Force nurse in northern Iraq and a Marine in
Baghdad said that God was there for them. "Like most persons, I had always
been skeptical about people seeing visions and hearing voices," writes E. B.
Sledge. "But I believe God spoke to me that night on the Peleliu battlefield."[4]
From that point, Sledge felt certain that he would survive.

Some warriors meet God for the first time in combat zones.[5] While preaching soldiers are mostly unwelcome, the rare Christian combatant of strong, obvious, and genuine faith can be an inspiration to others.[6] And while chaplains are
often criticized and dismissed by warriors, they can also, through their actions,

---

Some POWs who did not face the threat of torture felt neither burning hatred for the enemy nor a strong compulsion to consider theological matters.

2. William P. Mahedy, *Out of the Night: The Spiritual Journey of Vietnam Vets* (New
York: Ballantine Books, 1986), 4-5 and *passim*.

3. Wallace Terry, *Bloods: An Oral History of the Vietnam War by Black Veterans* (New
York: Ballantine Books, 1984), 30. Also see Uwe Siemon-Netto, *The Acquittal of God: A
Theology for Vietnam Veterans* (New York: Pilgrim Press, 1990), 45.

4. E. B. Sledge, *With the Old Breed: At Peleliu and Okinawa* (New York: Oxford University Press, 1981), 91.

5. Russell Cartwright Stroup, *Letters from the Pacific: A Combat Chaplain in World War
II*, ed., Richard Cartwright Austin (Columbia: University of Missouri Press, 2000), 142
and 151. Stroup relates an account of a captured Japanese Catholic making confession to
a Filipino priest, the service being conducted in Latin (195).

6. Of Corporal Ted Bishop, Bruce H. Norton, *Force Recon Diary, 1969* (New York: Ivy
Books, 1991) writes: "He was always happy and said that he found his happiness in reading and studying the Bible.... He was personally interested in each one of us, and his
interest was genuine" (124). See the appreciative comments on the wartime work of Father Albert Basil in William O. Darby and William H. Baumer, *We Led the Way: Darby's
Rangers* (New York: Presidio Press, 1980), 52. For commentary on a disinterest in evan-
gelism among soldiers in WWI, see Richard Schweitzer, *The Cross and the Trenches:
Religious Faith and Doubt among British and American Great War Soldiers* (Westport,
CT: Praeger, 2003), 196.

bring a sense of God's presence into a war zone. They do this, for example, by tending to the wounded in a firefight in the course of a mission they had no obligation to participate in. One chaplain in Vietnam walked voluntarily on a flight line when artillery was incoming to check on the men. Other chaplains have insisted on holding services in bombed out churches.[7]

Chaplains receive the highest praise when they unnecessarily put themselves into dangerous situations among warriors, when they risk and sometimes lose their lives helping the wounded and administering last rites while under fire. The researcher asked a Vietnam veteran, "What would Jesus have done in the battle for Hill 875?" He said Jesus would have done what Father Charles Watters did. Watters did not have to go the field; he was unarmed; and when the battle began he acted as a medic. He was killed by accidental friendly ordinance. "Would Father Watters have helped wounded North Vietnamese, too?" Without hesitation the veteran responded: "yes."[8]

With few exceptions, combat veterans say that God has nothing to do with war. Or, if God did have something to do with the wars of ancient Israel (this is mentioned often), the veterans still usually say that God did not have anything to do with the war *they* fought in. God is there for individuals within war, veterans say, but, so far as *they* know, he is not involved in the political or cultural problems that cause war.[9] There are some exceptions, of course. A tank operator in the Gulf War named his machine *Crusading for Christ*. But this pious effort was swamped by others tank names in the same company—*Phantom Lord*, *Stranger*, *Wolverine*, and *Coke Whore*.[10]

Most combat veterans say that war is man's problem and that God's interest is in the individual. God is "there" in battle in some general sense, but he is not

---

7. Vietnam veteran in discussion with Preston Jones, John Brown University, June 18, 2006. See Robert Tonsetic, *Warriors: An Infantryman's Memoir of Vietnam* (New York: Ballatine Books, 2004), 32; Edwin Campion Vaughn, *Some Desperate Glory: The World War I Diary of a British Officer, 1917* (New York: Henry Holt and Company, 1981), 184; and Stroup, *Letters from the Pacific*, 31, 42. More than their Protestant counterparts, Catholic chaplains speak specifically in terms of representing Christ among combatants. In Thomas O'Brien, *Blessings from the Battlefield* (Huntington, IN: Our Sunday Visitor Publishing, 2002), Father Jeldo J. Schiavone refers to his work in Vietnam as being "a Christ figure bringing comfort to the men of the battalion" (91).
8. Vietnam paratrooper in discussion with Preston Jones, John Brown University, June 16, 2006. See Berry F. Clifton, Jr., *Sky Soldiers: The Illustrated History of the Vietnam War* (New York: Bantam, 1987), 109. Stroup, *Letters from the Pacific*, writes about caring for enemy prisoners (45); and James Johnson, *Combat Chaplain: A Thirty-Year Vietnam Battle* (Denton, TX: University of North Texas Press, 2001), recalls praying for the family of a dead ("unlucky") Vietcong enemy (54).
9. For descriptions of very different experiences, see John Sack, *Company C: The Real War in Iraq* (New York: Avon Books, 1995), 152-153, 179-189. In discussions with the authors, a few WWII veterans said that they feel certain that, given the habitual atrocities of the Nazis and Japanese forces, God favored the Allies.
10. Sack, *Company C*, 93-4.

involved. "God is present without being interactive," says a veteran of Operation Iraqi Freedom. "God wants to make things better but people aren't letting him."[11] The researcher asked a retired Air Force veteran: "what would Jesus say if he were on the flight line in Da Nang when the Tet Offensive began?" The veteran responded, "He would say, 'I never knew you'"—meaning, Jesus would not have anything to say about the Tet Offensive; he would only have wanted to know where he stood in relation to the individual. The researcher asked a nurse what Jesus would say at the end of the worst day in the operating room at a hospital in Kirkuk, Iraq. "I don't think he'd say anything," she responded. "What do you say about things that ugly?" But she says she sensed Jesus telling her, "You're gonna be OK"—meaning, regardless of whatever is going on here, I care about you.[12]

Suppose there is a firefight in South Vietnam and Jesus is there. He walks back and forth, across the lines of fire; he whispers in the ears of the Americans and the Vietcong, "It's OK"—meaning, whatever you're doing now, I just care about you. *Does this*—the researcher asked one former combatant after another—*does this seem plausible, given what you have experienced of battle?* Unanimously, the veterans interviewed for this study who are Christians said "yes."[13] Their experience brings fresh meaning to the biblical idea that sometimes God's presence is not found in dramatic wind, earthquakes, and fire but in a still, small voice.[14] Their experience brings life to the psalmist's claim that even in *Sheol,* God is there.[15]

***

How can God both be and not be in the world of combat?

The reality Christian combat veterans describe, though not explicitly, is one in which the paperwork orderliness of military planning and organization exists alongside chaos, randomness, contingency, pain, and senselessness. Christian

---

11. Air Force nurse discussion with Preston Jones, Eagle River, Alaska, June 24, 2006.

12. In Kirkuk, Iraq, it would make sense to put a severely wounded insurgent aside for a while. But a Christian Air Force surgeon who was told this wondered, What if the roles were reversed? And he thought to himself: "Jesus heals people." Air Force surgeon in discussion with Preston Jones, Eagle River, Alaska, July 28, 2006

13. Christian veterans usually say that God does not take sides in war. See Lynn Hampton, *The Fighting Strength: Memoirs of a Combat Nurse in Vietnam* (New York: Warner Books, 1990), 227.

14. Allusions are to I Kings 19:11-12. Gordon makes this point in *To End All Wars*, 176.

15. Psalm 139:8b. The Old Testament concept of *sheol* differs from the New Testament's images of hell, but its associations with a netherworld, the realm of death, and a place with varying degrees of joy and torment correspond to the experiences of combat. For a brief entry on *Sheol*, see Daid Lyle Jeffrey, *A Dictionary of Biblical Tradition in English Literature* (Grand Rapids: Eerdmans, 1992), 710. On former combatants wanting "to find God in the midst of hell" see William P. Mahedy, *Out of the Night: The Spiritual Journey of Vietnam Vets* (New York: Ballantine Books, 1986), 127.

combatants relate their belief in a God who presides over the world in a general way and yet, in the context of war, allows for seemingly unmitigated freedom. For many Christian veterans, God seems absent from the world of war—yet they believe he has an overriding plan.

So the domain of combat is perplexing: God is not there *and* he is there; sometimes (in a small number of cases) his presence is keenly felt,[16] though veterans have a difficult time saying *how* God was present.

These confusing experiences contribute to the sense that war is abnormal, that its essence is beyond the boundaries of describable reality. Some veterans liken combat to a dream state or to a kind of out-of-body experience.[17] But to read the history of humankind, or to scan the newspaper, is to be confronted with the rhetorical question, Is there anything more normal than war?[18] The point gains strength if we think of war metaphorically and consider the battles academics, neighbors, religious denominations, political persuasions, family members, ethnic groups, tribes, celebrities, and sports fans wage on one another.[19] Perhaps most people need look no farther than their own souls to gain insight into the way conflict pervades human life.[20]

In this, people resemble the natural world of which they are a part: made *in* God's image but *of* dust.[21] And the world combat veterans describe resembles the universe theologically-informed scientists (and scientifically-informed theologians) describe. Maybe this is because the description of the natural world as being "rife with happenstance, contingency, incredible waste, death, pain and horror" could easily be applied to the world of combat. And when a scientist who is not a Christian says that a God who created such a world is not one people would want to pray to, he is echoing the sentiment of some combatants.[22]

---

16. WWII veteran in discussion with Preston Jones, John Brown University, June 6, 2006.

17. Discussions with veterans of Vietnam and Iraqi Freedom. A soldier at My Lai said afterwards: "That is not me. Something happened to me." Quoted in Jonathan Glover, *Humanity: A Moral History of the Twentieth Century* (New Haven: Yale University Press, 1999), 61.

18. See the chapter "War is Normal" in James Hillman, *A Terrible Love of War* (New York: Penguin Press, 2004). Hillman writes: "During the five thousand six hundred years of written history, fourteen thousand six hundred wars have been recorded. Two or three wars for each of year human history" (17).

19. As Sigmund Freud saw: "men [i.e. human beings] are not gentle creatures...they are, on the contrary, creatures among whose instinctual endowments is to be reckoned a powerful share of aggressiveness.... It is clearly not easy for men to give up the satisfaction of this inclination to aggression. They do not feel comfortable without it. *Civilization and Its Discontents* (1930) excerpted in Marvin Perry, ed., *Sources of the Western Tradition* vol. II (Boston: Houghton Mifflin Company, 2006), 164-5

20. St. Paul makes the point in Romans 7:19-24.

21. Genesis 2:7.

22. David Hull quoted in John Haught, *God after Darwin: A Theology of Evolution* (Boulder: Westview Press, 2000), 6.

Since, in ways, the worlds of war and nature resemble one another in their redness of tooth and claw, it makes sense to draw on the work of scientists who take up theological questions, for their theology is driven by what they see in the natural world.[23] And what the students of nature who are cited below see is something like what Christian combatants see: a world in which "God interacts with the world but is not in total control of all its [processes]"[24]—not because he is the supreme being of the Enlightenment deists (a one-time creator now uninvolved), and not because he is weak and unable to maintain control of everything, but because allowing another entity (nature, a person) to be completely itself means giving that being real freedom—the kind of freedom combat veterans suggest exists in the world of war.

This study is not the place to enjoin the ancient argument over the extent to which people's actions are free or determined. The point here is only to say that the view expressed by prominent scientists from different Christian denominations who think about God's interaction with the world are attractive to a person contemplating the question of God's place in a world of war. It is tedious to cite one lengthy quotation after another, but in this case the point is best made that way.

Consider "God's relative hiddenness in creation," an astrophysicist writes. "God has created and is creating it, but at the same time is radically setting it free to become itself, to discover itself, to become conscious of itself, to become free."[25] And physicist John Polkinghorne writes:

> The actual balance between chance and necessity, contingency and potentiality, which we perceive seems to me to be consistent with the will of a patient and subtle Creator, content to achieve his purpose through the unfolding of process and accepting thereby a measure of the vulnerability and precariousness which always characterize the gift of freedom by love.[26]

Physical chemist Arthur Peacocke detects something similar. "[I]ndependence and freedom are an inevitable consequence of the very self-consciousness that has emerged naturalistically," he writes. "We cannot help concluding that God

---

23. For example, Polkinghorne, *Faith of a Physicist* (Minneapolis: Fortress Press, 1996), 1-6.
24. Ibid., 81.
25. "Describing God's Action," in Robert John Russell et al., eds., *Chaos and Complexity: Scientific Perspectives on Divine Action* (Vatican City: Vatican Observatory Foundation, 2000), 260.
26. John Polkinghorne, *One World: The Interaction of Science and Theology* (Princeton: Princeton University Press, 1986), 69. Also see the similar statement made in Polkinghorne's *Faith, Science, and Understanding* (New Haven: Yale University Press, 2000), 111.

intended that out of matter persons should evolve who had ... freedom, and thereby allowed the possibility that they might depart from God's intentions.[27]

And so on:

> We are material beings with an independent physical existence, and to fashion such beings, a Creator would have had to produce an independent material universe in which our evolution over time was a contingent possibility. A believer in the divine accepts God's love and His gifts of freedom are genuine—so genuine that they include the power to choose evil and, if we wish, to freely send ourselves to hell. (Kenneth Miller, cell biologist)[28]

And, somewhat differently:

> Ours is a world of love and ecstatic joy, but also a world of suffering and excruciating pain. It is not a world of all or none, but a [complex] world, where chance and randomness join with choice and inexorable law. (Owen Gingerich, astronomer)[29]

These quotations do not prove anything theological; after two millennia of debate, it seems doubtful that a definitive argument about human freedom, or the lack of it, could be made in such a way as to please all interested parties.[30] It is striking, though, that scientists who start from the "bottom up"—who, to one extent or another, derive their theological reflection from what they know about the operations of nature—emphasize existential freedom, as do veterans who have experienced the facts of war.[31]

Combat veterans focus on human freedom, it seems, because a free world can accommodate the contingency, randomness, and pain that pervade both

---

27. Arthur Peacocke, *Paths from Science towards God: The End of All Our Exploring* (Oxford: Oneworld, 2001), 89.
28. Kenneth Miller, *Finding Darwin's God: A Scientist's Search for Common Ground Between God and Evolution* (New York: HarperCollins, 1999), 291.
29. Owen Gingerich, *God's Universe* (Cambridge: Harvard Universty Press, 2006), 119-20.
30. The point is made well in John Kekes, *Pluralism in Philosophy: Changing the Subject* (Ithaca: Cornell University Press, 2000), 103-23.
31. See Siemon-Netto, *Acquittal of God*, 65-6. Also see, Mahedy, *Out of the Night*, 224-5. Theological libertarianism also has the support of theologians and Christian philosophers of different confessional stripes. See, for example, Richard Swinburne, *The Christian God* (Oxford: Clarendon Press, 1994), 152; William Hasker, *God, Time, and Knowledge* (Ithaca: Cornell University Press, 1989); Paul S. Fiddes, *The Creative Suffering of God* (Oxford: Clarendon Press, 1988), 33 and 92; Clark Pinnock et al., *The Openness of God* (Downers Grove, IL: InterVarsity Press, 1994); Gregory A. Boyd, *God of the Possible: A Biblical Introduction to the Open View of God* (Grand Rapids, MI: Baker Books, 2000); and John Sanders, *The God Who Risks: A Theology of Providence* (Downers Grove, IL: InterVarsity Press, 1996).

combat and the natural world. It is true that an unfree world presided over by capricious gods who inflict humankind with tragedy, the way boys inflict wanton harm on insects, can also accommodate the realties of combat, but that is not what the Christian God is like.[32] "I couldn't understand how a good God could allow innocent people ... to suffer so horribly," wrote a nurse after her experience in Vietnam. But later she came to see that "God literally made men free—free even to sin and hurt one another if they so desire."[33]

If, as one scholar puts it, a theological view too concerned with order is unable to cope with the realities of natural history, such a theology is also unable to cope with the randomness and chaos of warfare.[34] The idea that people are free—*truly*, not just apparently—to do as they choose mitigates the problem war veterans see in the claim that God controls all things.

But is God so powerless that he is unable or unwilling to step in for the sake of people? Could not God have done *something* to prevent that heroic priest on Hill 875 from being immolated by napalm dropped by pilots on his own side?[35]

One answer is that God *has* done something. Christians believe that the passion, death, and resurrection of Jesus make war unnecessary. Jesus says, "Peace I leave with you, my peace I give unto you."[36] But the cross also means that God takes the rejection of Himself to Himself. If people will not accept the liberty God offers, he will still abide with them.[37] God "will not leave you as orphans."[38] The cross is the way out and the symbol of God's identification with those who do not, or for some reason cannot, accept it. The cross paves the way for Christ's own descent into hell and symbolizes his conquest over all that makes hell possible.[39]

The way of the cross is the way of salvation, personally—but also culturally and politically, if somehow all the world would follow Jesus. But Jesus knew that all the world would not follow him, and he knew that those who claimed, and still claim, to follow him do so poorly—even, as has been obvious in history, to the point of waging war in his name.[40] But this refusal does not make the

---

32. The allusion is to the words of Gloucester in Shakespeare's *King Lear:* "As flies to wanton boys, are we to the gods; They kill us for their sport" (scene iv, act I, lines 37-38).
33. Hampton, *Fighting Strength,* 211 and 214. Also see Andrew Exum, *This Man's Army: A Soldier's Story from the Front Lines of the War on Terrorism* (New York: Gotham, 2005), 234; and Mahedy, *Out of the Night,* 154.
34. In *God after Darwin*, Haught writes: "A theology obsessed with order is ill prepared for evolution" (5).
35. Vietnam paratrooper veteran in discussion with Preston Jones, John Brown University, June 18, 2006.
36. John 14:27a.
37. Siemon-Netto, *Acquittal of God*, quotes Paul Tillich: "When the Divine is rejected, It takes rejection upon Itself" (41).
38. John 14:18.
39. Karl Rahner, *On the Theology of Death* (New York: Herder and Herder, 1961), 63-4.
40. See, for example, John 15:18-26 and I Corinthians 6:1-11.

cross irrelevant, for in the cross we see Jesus suffering with a humanity that has brought so much trouble on itself.

The crucifixion of Jesus is a discrete historical event—the event, as the New Testament repeatedly says, that makes possible salvation and new life in Christ.[41] But the cross also has meaning for the man in combat whose thoughts are far from God, who feels abandoned by God, who finds everything he has been told about God thrown into question.

The engaged warrior has no time to contemplate deep questions, and the death of Jesus at a particular moment on a particular day two millennia ago is as irrelevant to him as everything else not directly related to surviving a barrage, a walk through a minefield, an ambush, or an airlift of the wounded under fire. But if the crucifixion is more than one event—if it is also "a revelation of the order of reality," then its relevance to the man in combat becomes clear.[42]

The crucifixion means that God's suffering on the cross was caused *by* people but also that he suffered *for* people. And if it is the case that the Son of God was "slain before the foundation of the world" (that is, it is eternal past), and if it is true that the Son of God can, in some sense, be crucified again and again as a result of sin (that is, it is present and future), then the cross suggests that God also suffers in time.[43] This is a suffering that corresponds to the pain that people feel and cause.[44]

There is, as one theologian has said, an "eternal cross in the heart of God,"[45] and when Holocaust survivor Elie Wiesel says that Auschwitz "murdered his God," the Christian sees that Wiesel is stating a truth, albeit not a final truth.[46]

---

41. Perhaps the clearest statement is found in John 3:16.

42. H. Richard Neibuhr, "War as Crucifixion" in Richard B. Miller, ed., *War in the Twentieth Century: Sources in Theological Ethics* (Louisville: Westminister/John Knox Press, 1992), 69.

43. In the early fourth century, St. Jerome wrote: "Every day Christ is crucified, for we [Christians] are crucified to the world, and Christ is crucified in us. Blessed is the one in whose heart Christ rises every day because every day such a one does penance even for the smallest sins." See J. Robert Wright, ed., *Readings for the Daily Office from the Early Church* (New York: Church Publishing Incorporated, 1991), 168.

44. The biblical references are to Revelation 13:8 and Hebrews 6:6. In *Chance and Providence: God's Action in a World Governed by Scientific Law* (New York: Charles Scribner's Sons, 1958), William G. Pollard writes: "[The] Biblical view of God's action and man's freedom rises to its most decisive and conclusive peak in the great and climactic event of Calvary. There in the humble nobility of the lonely figure of the 'Word made flesh and dwelt among us' in the presence of the howling mob shouting with hot and bitter anger for His crucifixion, we see the terrible reality of human freedom at its worst. Here 'Him by whom all things were made,' even the creator and preserver of those who now press Him so hotly, is Himself the object of the most passionate desire for evil that human freedom can choose" (133).

45. Quoted in Fiddes, *The Creative Suffering of God*, 29.

46. Elie Wiesel, *Night* (New York: Bantam Books, 1960), 32. Later, after an execution, a prisoner in Auschwitz asks where God is. "I heard a voice within me answer," Wiesel writes: "'Where is He? Here He is—He is hanging here on this gallows'" (62). A few

For the soldier's agony, loneliness, and loss of morale are also God's; "the suffering of men finds its extension in that of their Creator."[47] William Mahedy, who served as a chaplain in Vietnam, writes that his war was "all about the cross"—death, despair and sin confronted by new life, forgiveness and hope.[48] The same could, perhaps, be said of all wars. "The Crucifixion ... told us," a Second World War POW wrote, "that God was in our midst, suffering with us."[49]

An excellent study of the religious lives of American and British combatants in the First World War reveals the extent to which warriors interpreted their experience in relation to the cross. As one fighter put it, the crucifixes soldiers often saw in France brought to their minds the "broken figure of Christ brooding over a world that was denying him." Reflecting on a crucifix that was intact after a battle, a soldier named Conignsby Dawson wrote:

> The Christ upon His Cross is still untouched, though the shrine and surrounding trees are smashed to atoms. I think He means more to me like that—stripped of his gorgeousness—than ever. He seems so like ourselves in His lonely and unhallowed suffering.[50]

A chaplain wrote about a soldier who was not religious but who, in his grief, had been driven to consider the suffering of Christ. A British veteran remembered soldiers "on the road to Calvary" singing "[General] *Kitchener Loves Me, this I know, 'cos the Bible tells me so*"; another warrior prayed the Stations of the Cross everyday in order to bring the war to an end.[51] And so on:

> Nature shows us a spirit, not like a King on a throne who has only to lift his finger to get things done, but a spirit very like Christ upon the Cross, Who had to suffer agony to get things done, but Who gets them done, because He is patient and persists.

---

years before the Second World War, Reinhold Niebuhr wrote that "pure goodness, without power, cannot maintain itself in the world. It ends on the cross. Yet that is not where it finally ends. The Messiah will transmute the whole world order." See Niebuhr's *Beyond Tragedy: Essays on the Christian Interpretation of History* (New York: Charles Scribner's Sons, 1937), 177-8.

47. Elie Wiesel, *All Rivers Run to the Sea: Memoirs* (New York: Schocken Books, 1995), 103. Fiddes, in *The Creative Suffering of God*, quotes Horace Bushnell who, the year after the American Civil War ended (1866) wrote: "It is as if there were a cross unseen, standing on its undiscovered hill, far back in the ages, out of which there were sounding always just the same deep voice of suffering love and patience that was heard by mortal ears from the sacred hill of calvary" (29).

48. Mahedy, *Out of the Night*, 168-169.

49. Gordon, *To End All Wars*, 119.

50. Schweitzer, *Cross and the Trenches*, 22, 28.

51. Ibid., 19, 29, 36. Kitchener replaces Jesus in the popular children's Sunday school song.

The church ... was a deplorable sight.... Nothing stood except one thing—a cross with the crucified Christ nailed to it *alone* remained. I saw that cross and wondered. Everything mutilated, and yet that cross still stood. It seemed to be a message of Hope. 'He that believes in me shall *never* die.'

I had had a vision of Christ with extended arms in front of us ... and instead of bearing all our sins, He was bearing all the harm from the shells.

What has depressed me more than anything else [are] the Crucifixes one occasionally sees standing in desolate shell-swept areas. The horror of the one intensifies a hundred-fold that of the other, and the image of the tortured Christ strikes one as an appalling monument to the Personification of Utter Failure. [52]

***

In the depths of the Second World War, H. Richard Niebuhr reflected on the theme of war as crucifixion. Niebuhr's essay is abstract; he refers to his own thoughts as "vague gestures" toward a theory of war as crucifixion;[53] his ideas are far removed from the experiences of combatants. But, like the words that construe war as hell, the language of crucifixion appears too frequently in war memoirs to be dismissed as only the stuff of metaphor and cultural memory.

Warriors speak of the shedding of blood for the benefit of others and of dying for a cause greater than oneself; they speak of combatants being men of sorrows who are acquainted with grief.[54] Fighters commend themselves into the hands of God; they resign themselves to his inscrutable will.[55] One soldier saw a wounded comrade who looked like a "suffering Christ," whose loss was a "blood sacrifice."[56] An officer spoke of his own soldiers and the enemy as having paid the price for the world's sins. The soldiers' task, he said, was to purge the sin with "blood-offerings."[57]

Men make the sign of the cross before going into combat, and the scorching thirst combatants feel recalls the hours of Calvary.[58] The importance of communion—the Eucharist—to combatants points to their identification with Jesus'

---

52. Ibid., 39, 45, 49, 210.
53. Niebuhr, "War as Crucifixion," 70.
54. Mahedy, *Out of the Night*, 182. The biblical allusion is to Isaiah 53:3.
55. The biblical allusions are to (among others) Luke 22:20 and 42; Luke 23:46.
56. Witkop, *German Students' War Letters*, 23-4, 59, 81, 91, 204, 235, 268, 316, 330, 356.
57. Joshua Lawrence Chamberlain, *Passing of the Armies* (New York: Barnes and Noble, 2004), 198.
58. On thirst, see, for example, Sledge, *With the Old Breed,* 75; Caputo, *Rumor of War*, 22; and Johnson, *Combat Chaplain*, 55.

sacrifice. Among the broken bodies of battle, warriors take to themselves the broken body of Jesus.[59]

Sometimes warriors, like Pilate under duress, want to wash their hands of the blood of war.[60] And wartime reflections can sound like what might have been said at a mid-twentieth-century Golgotha:

> Nearby our regimental Protestant chaplain had set up a little altar made out of a box from which he was administering Holy Communion to a small group of dirty Marines. I glanced at the face of a Marine opposite me.... He was filthy like all of us.... He watched the chaplain with an expression of skepticism that seemed to ask, "What's the use of all that? Is it gonna keep them guys from getting hit?" That face was so weary but so expressive that I knew he, like all of us, couldn't help but have doubts about [the chaplains'] God in the presence of the constant shock and suffering. Why did it go on and on?[61]

More explicit are the words of Tim O'Brien:

> This morning, coming out of a hooch, I watched as a junior officer literally kicked a Vietnamese woman out of the company area adjacent to ours. I watched. The observer, the peeping tom of this army. Doing nothing. I was suddenly sickened by the thought of the near two thousand years that separate my life and that of a Roman centurion who stood by a narrow alley leading to Golgotha and who also watched, doing nothing. What difference then? What earthly change have centuries of suffering and joy wrought? Is it only that Christ is become a yellow-skinned harlot, a Sunday-morning short-time girl?[62]

Another veteran recalls seeing two young girls nailed to posts, "sacrificed like Vietnamese Jesuses."[63]

Philip Caputo likened his duties as an officer to the Stations of the Cross, writing bitterly that

> [i]n Vietnam men died at calvaries named Hamburger Hill and the Rockpile, but they had no chance of resurrection—of being raised again in the nation's proud memories; no chance of redemption, except that their memory might "prevent the next generation from being crucified in the next war."[64]

---

59. "With the smell of our dead buddies, stacked in empty bunkers, still in our noses," one veteran recalled, "[the priest] walked among us with another broken body." Quoted in Siemon-Netto, *Acquittal of God*, 54.

60. Mahedy, *Out of the Night*, 13.

61. Sledge, *With the Old Breed*, 242.

62. Tim O'Brien, *If I Die in a Combat Zone*, 183. Earlier O'Brien writes about three elderly detainees: "They were only a few feet away, hanging to their saplings like the men at Golgotha" (133).

63. Turnipseed, *Baghdad Express*, 191.

64. Caputo, *Rumor of War*, xxi and 232.

In one way or another, the cross punctuates the world of war. A Marine saw it in the way a machine gunner braces his weapon across the back of his shoulders with his hands draping over its butt and muzzle.[65] A nurse haunted by experiences of war slept gripping a crucifix.[66] A Catholic chaplain endangered himself to procure a crucifix for his chapel.[67] Combatants gathered for communion "in remembrance of Him whose body was broken and whose blood was shed."[68] A chaplain wondered if in some way he could be a Simon to the troops, to ease "the burden of the cross" that was heavy on them.[69] A poignant description of the crucifixion comes from an atheist Marine setting an evangelistic comrade straight on what bearing one's cross in battle means. "It's a heavy load," he writes:

> And it's uphill and people spit on you and you have these thorns digging into your skull and blood and sweat dripping in your eyes, and all this struggle is so you can carry yourself up to your death, to the scene where your father will forsake you.[70]

In the crucifixion, the Christian combatant caught up in war can see that war is unnecessary; he can see that the cross is the way to peace.[71] But the cross also shows that God suffers with the pain of this troubled creation.[72] John Polkinghorne writes about the pain of the natural world, but his comments are relevant here. The burden of suffering in the world seems to cast doubt on the idea of a loving God, he writes, but

> [a]t the deepest level I believe that the only possible answer is to be found in the darkness and dereliction of the cross, where Christianity asserts that in the lonely figure hanging there we see God himself opening his arms to embrace the bitterness of the strange world he has made.[73]

---

65. Ibid., 96.
66. Hampton, *Fighting Strength*, 212.
67. Bob Stoffey, *Cleared Hot! The Diary of a Marine Combat Pilot in Vietnam* (New York: St. Martin's Paperbacks, 1992), 66-84.
68. Stroup, *Letters from the Pacific*, 178.
69. Ibid., 178.
70. Turnipseed, *Baghdad Express*, 83.
71. Reinhold Niebuhr, *Faith and History: A Comparison of Christian and Modern Views of History* (New York: Charles Scribner's Sons, 1949), 143-4.
72. Augustine, Anselm, Aquinas, and Calvin denied that God suffers, but in recent decades an increasing number of theologians have come to see that the belief in the impassability of God (i.e. of God's inability to suffer) is more akin to Platonic philosophy than to the biblical record. See Fiddes, *Creative Suffering of God*, 17-18.
73. Polkinghorne, *One World*, 80. Haught, *God after Darwin*, makes a similar point: "Reflection on the Darwinian world can lead us to contemplate more explicitly the mystery of God as it is made manifest in the story of life's suffering, the epitome of which lies for Christians in the crucifixion of Jesus. In the symbol of the cross, Christian belief discovers a God who participates fully in the world's struggle and pain" (46).

The combatant can envision Christ's arms still stretched on the cross—despite dubious causes and fanaticism, self-deception and grandiosity, brutality and misguided senses of honor. And he can see that Christ's arms are outstretched for the Vietcong guerilla and U.S. naval officer, for the man on patrol and the insurgent, for the helicopter pilot and combat medic. Perhaps the combatant can understand better than most the petition in the Book of Common Prayer:

> Lord Jesus Christ, who didst stretch out thine arms of love on the hard wood of the cross that everyone might come within reach of thy saving embrace; So clothe us in thy Spirit that we, reaching forth our hands in love, may bring those who do not know thee to the knowledge and love of thee; for the honor of thy name. *Amen.* [74]

Thus we come to another scandal of the cross, a scandal detected by Abraham Lincoln—that great theologian of the American Civil War—and repeated since: namely, God's refusal to declare which side he is on, or even to take sides. [75] The suffering of the American or Australian POW in a Japanese camp is God's, and the suffering of a Japanese soldier starving to death on an island surrounded by the Allies is also God's. Jesus suffers with the teenage sniper who has taken down another enemy, and he suffers with the human target. Jesus suffers in war because the cross makes the agony of war unnecessary; and he suffers because wars are what creatures in a free world wage. He will not abandon people, so he suffers with them when they are at their worst, or when they are responding in battle to events over which they have no control. All along, the emblem of God's suffering with people also points the way out of the suffering. The cross is curse and cure.

But even in his identification with the suffering people bring on themselves—even in his hiddenness, in his seeming absence in the world of battle—God draws people. The combat warrior, who carries the consequences of the sins of tribes and nations, can understand something of what the cross means. In the words of one combat chaplain, from the vantage point of "the cross on which

---

74. The Office of Morning Prayer, *Book of Common Prayer*, 1977, rite 1. Notice that Christ's action (the first part of the prayer) is not contingent on the petitioners' "reaching forth" of their own hands. Mahedy, *Out of the Night*, discusses one veteran who "feels that he has a better understanding of the cross of Christ after Vietnam" (129).

75. A powerful feature of Lincoln's Second Inaugural Address (1865), which strikes Mark Noll for its "theological depth," is the president's refusal to assume that God was on the side of the North in the American Civil War. The war, Lincoln said, was God's judgment on the entire country. See Noll's, *America's God: From Jonathan Edwards to Abraham Lincoln* (Oxford: Oxford University Press, 2002), 434-6. During the Second World War, Chaplain Stroup reflected on Lincoln's words, saying that he uttered them with "the sign of the cross in his eyes." See *Letters from the Pacific*, 147-8. For a contemporary statement on this theme, see Felton May and Bob Edgar, "In war, you can't count God to be on your side," *Arkansas Democrat Gazette*, October 1, 2006, 2J. Also see, Mahedy, *Out of the Night*, 157.

they hang," combatants are able to see more deeply into the meaning of "that other Cross where goodness, justice, mercy, beauty, honor, and love are crucified."[76] And when, during the American Civil War, a wounded soldier asked the poet Walt Whitman to read to him, it seemed appropriate to the poet to read about the crucifixion. The soldier appreciated this, but wanted Whitman to keep reading—to read about the resurrection that overcame death.[77]

Now we consider an ancient soldier—a centurion—a man of battle—who found himself at the foot of a cross. Notice that the centurion whose words are recorded in the Gospels discovers the truth about Jesus at precisely the moment when, so far as anyone could tell, God was most distant. "My God, why have you forsaken me?" says Jesus. But the centurion says: "truly this man was the son of God."

Jesus is forsaken; the Roman soldier is found.[78] God is *not* there, yet he *is* there.[79] God's absence is accompanied by a haunting presence. God desires not to let people go.[80]

But what about just war theory? Or the pacifism of the Sermon on the Mount? How to reconcile the brutality of portions of the Old Testament with the peaceful, self-sacrificial mission of Jesus? These are important questions, but they mean little or nothing to a young man under fire, who is himself sacrificing because of, for, and with a fallen world.

Instead, we end with the testimony of a prisoner of war who suffered more than most combatants have or will, and who cursed an absent God. But, in time, he heard a small voice, and he saw his own complicity in the trouble of the world and its wars. Starving, weak, tortured, and diseased, he and his fellow prisoners saw that their lives on the horizontal plane of life were made meaningful only in relation to a crucifixion in a backwater of the Roman Empire, in all its loss, abandonment, humiliation, betrayal, and seeming pointlessness. For him, God's absence led to God's discovery.

"At the point marked by the Cross," the POW writes, "we found ourselves."[81]

---

76. Stroup, *Letters from the Pacific*, 206.
77. Walt Whitman, *Memoranda During the War*, ed., Pete Coviello (New York: Oxford University Press, 1990), 36.
78. See Mark 15:33-39.
79. In the epilogue to *God's Universe*, Gingerich reflects on God's interaction with the world and writes that Jesus' moment of dereliction made the nature of God's self-limitation in this world "excruciatingly clear" (121).
80. Mahedy, *Out of the Night*, 181.
81. Gordon, *To End All Wars*, 73, 77, 176, and 185.

Conclusion

Over time, Christian views on warfare have been various and complicated. For Tertullian, whose life spanned the latter second and early third centuries, the matter seemed simple. "Shall it be held lawful to make an occupation of the sword," he asked, "when the Lord proclaims that he who uses the sword shall perish by the sword?" The early theologian Origen took a similar view. He observed that Jesus "nowhere teaches that it is right for His own disciples to offer violence to any one, however wicked." Thirteen hundred years later, Menno Simons made the point this way: "Peter was commanded to sheathe his sword. All Christians are commanded to love their enemies; to do good unto those who abuse and persecute them; to give the mantle when the cloak is taken, the other cheek when one is struck."[1] These thinkers saw that it was impossible to envision Jesus fighting for a worldly cause, so how could his disciples do so?

Other Christian intellectuals have said that a Christian's involvement in war is justified if a war's cause is justified. Augustine saw that, sometimes, peace could be gained only through war, and he argued that "war should be waged only as a necessity." Even when prosecuting battle, Augustine continued, the Christian soldier should "cherish the spirit of a peacemaker." In the sixteenth century, Luther noted that God used the "sword" in war to punish evildoers the way police powers punish criminals in society. Thus, somewhat grimly: "the hand that wields this sword and kills with it is not man's hand, but God's; and it is not man, but God, who hangs, tortures, beheads, kills, and fights. All these are God's works and judgments." Calvin cautioned Christian combatants not to allow "themselves to be carried away by any private motive" but to be "wholly guided by public spirit"—by a genuine desire to defend the weak, to put down rebellion, punish crime, and to preserve tranquility.[2]

Erasmus of Rotterdam, Luther's and Calvin's contemporary (though not a Protestant) could also see that war might sometimes be justifiable but only as a last resort, when prosecuted with as little bloodshed as possible, and with an understanding that the message of the Prince of Peace and the world of war seemed to be fundamentally at odds. And even just wars could be disastrous. Erasmus envisioned victors weeping over victories "bought too dearly"; he peered into the damage combat could do to a person's soul. War might sometimes be necessary, Erasmus suggested, but it can never be good.[3]

---

1. Arthur F. Holmes, ed., *War and Christian Ethics: Classic Readings on the Morality of War* (Grand Rapids: Baker Book House, 1991), 45, 48, 186.
2. Ibid., 63, 143, 167-8.
3. Ibid., 177-84.

A few years after the Second World War, Reinhold Niebuhr would add to Christian reflection on war a note of frank realism made possible by the failure of optimistic views on human affairs. "In its profoundest insights," Niebuhr wrote, "the Christian faith sees the whole of human history as involved in guilt, and finds no release from guilt except in the grace of God." Even when people are acting on their best motivations, the blindness and darkness of the human condition are present. In some sense, Niebuhr wrote, "every man...is a crucifier of Christ."[4]

The study of combat adds force to Niebuhr's words. The Nazis' cause was evil, the GI's cause was to end that evil; but as human beings, Nazis and GIs were both guilty—for everyone has a part in the problems that lead to war. The Nazi bequeathed to his children and grandchildren a burden of shame and the GI came in time to be numbered among America's "greatest generation." Yet it is striking that war memoirs from victor and vanquished have so much in common. Combat veterans who know that they played a role in bringing down Hitler's evil regime still say that war is hell. The German film *Downfall* focuses on the collapse of Berlin in the spring of 1945; the American film *Saving Private Ryan* depicts American Rangers in France, killing Germans and helping to make Germany's collapse possible. But the films *feel* the same. Being on the winning side does not stop combat from being a nightmare.

Niebuhr's point is taken. Every person, in one way or another, is a crucifier of Christ. Warriors, perhaps like the centurion at Golgotha, know this better than anyone.

---

4. Ibid., 302, 312.

Bibliography[1]

Archival Materials

Oral History Project, National Museum of the Pacific War, Fredericksburg, Texas; unpublished interview manuscripts: George Allen Barrett; Helen Beattie; Frank H. Bigelow; Jay Bollmen; R. Thomas Bousman; Bill Brenner; John B. Brush; John Bumgartner; Frank Cabiness; Earle M. Craig; Dorothy Still Danner; Rudolph David; Herman Dupont; William R. Eoff; Eli Escobar; Linton H. Estes, Jr.; Fred Fox; Elmer Freeman; Frank Fujita; John Lo Gerfo; Margaret Gillooly; Elmer Graham; J. S. Gray; Elaine Graydon; John W. Griffing; Vernon Hanks; Dick Harrelson; Jack H. Heinzel; Raymond F. Higgins; Willie Higgs; Raymond F. Holloran; Don Innis; Clinton Jennings; Gunner O. Johnson; Bill Kapp; John Kidd; Jay Kopkey; Harry Litzelfelner; Jacqueline H. Lucas; Glen McDole; Orlyn Master; Andrew Miller; Ethel "Sally" Blaine Millett; Floyd C. Mumme; Gerald "Jerry" Munson; Lawrence Norris; Glenn S. Oliver; Alvin Orsland; Georgia Payne; George B. Raffield; Carey Randall; Jacqueline Nicol Raymond; John Ream; Everett D. Reamer; Walter Riley; Elliott Ross; Jay Rye; Richard Salter; Jim Slaughter; Neville Stopford; Albert Taylor; Lester Tenney; Kyle Thompson; Ken Towery; Hershel Woodrow Williams; R. Murphy Williams

Books, Articles, Documentaries, Films

Adams, Virginia M., ed. *On the Altar of Freedom: A Black Soldier's Civil War Letters from the Front.* New York: Warner Books, 1991.

Adler, Bill, ed. *Letters from Vietnam.* New York: Ballantine Books, 2003.

Alexievich, Svetlana. *Zinky Boys: Soviet Voices from the Afghanistan War.* Translated by Julia and Robin Whitby. New York: W. W. Norton Company, 1992.

Ambush in Mogadishu. VHS. Directed by William Cran. Frontline-PBS; WGBH Boston, 1998.

Anderson Platoon, The. VHS. Directed by Pierre Schoendoerffer. Homevision, 2000.

---

1. In addition to the sources listed in the bibliography, underpinning this study are background interviews and conversations with combat veterans conducted by the authors between 1997 and 2008. The authors interviewed: 33 veterans of the Second World War; 3 veterans of the Korean conflict; 20 veterans of the Vietnam conflict; 2 veterans of operations Desert Shield/Desert Storm; 4 veterans of the anti-terrorism effort in Afghanistan; and 8 veterans of the operations in Iraq, 2003-2008.

"Atheists in Foxholes Speeches." *Atheists In Foxholes.* http://www.atheistfoxholes.org/ speeches.php (accessed 10 October 2006).

Augustine. *Concerning the City of God against the Pagans.* Translated by Henry Bettenson. New York: Penguin Books, 1984.

Bad Voodoo's War. TV. Directed by Deborah Scranton. Frontline-PBS; WGBH, Boston, 2008.

Baillie, John. "Morning Prayers." In Foster and Smith, *Devotional Classics,* 108-14.

Barbusse, Henri. *Under Fire.* Translated by Robin Buss. New York: Penguin, 2004.

Bassett, John T. *War Journal of an Innocent Soldier.* New York: Avon Books, 1989.

Battle of the Bulge. VHS. Directed by Ken Annakin. Boston, MA: WGBH BostonVideo. 2002.

Behâ-ed-Din. "Richard I Massacres Prisoners after Taking Acre, 2-20 August 1191." In Carey, *Eyewitness to History,* 35-37.

Bennett, Donald V. *Honor Untarnished: A West Point Graduate's Memoir of World War II.* New York: Forge, 2003.

Berstein, Alan E. *The Formation of Hell: Death and Retribution in the Ancient and Early Christian Worlds.* Ithaca: Cornell University Press, 1993.

Bidermann, Gottlob Herbert. *In Deadly Combat: A German Soldier's Memoir of the Eastern Front.* Translated by Derek S. Zumbro. Lawrence: University Press of Kansas, 2000.

Bitton-Jackson, Livia. *I Have Lived a Thousand Years: Growing Up in the Holocaust.* New York: Simon Pulse, 1997.

Black Hawk Down. DVD. Directed by Ridley Scott. Columbia TriStar Home Enter-Taiment, 2002.

Blumenson, Martin, ed. *The Patton Papers: 1940-1945.* Boston: Houghton Mifflin Co., 1974.

Boot, Max. *The Savage Wars of Peace: Small Wars and the Rise of American Power.* New York: Basic Books, 2002.

Borgman, Dean. *Hear My Story: Understanding the Cries of Troubled Youth.* Peabody, MA: Hendrickson Publishers, 2003.

Borovik, Artyom. *The Hidden War: A Russian Journalist's Account of the Soviet War in Afghanistan.* New York: Grove Press, 1990.

Bourke, Joanna. *An Intimate History of Killing.* London: Granta Books, 1999.

Bowden, Mark. *Black Hawk Down*. New York: Penguin Books, 2000.

Boyd, Gregory A. *God of the Possible: A Biblical Introduction to the Open View of God*. Grand Rapids: Baker Books, 2000.

Boyington, Gregory. *Baa Baa Black Sheep*. New York: Bantam Books, 1977.

Boyle, Jerome M. *Apache Sunrise*. New York: Ivy Books, 1994.

Brittain, Vera. *Testament of Youth: An Autobiographical Study of the Years, 1900-1925*. New York: Penguin Books, 1978.

Britton, Wiley. *Memoirs of the Rebellion on the Border, 1863*. Lincoln: University of Nebraska Press, 1993.

Buttrick, George A. "A Simple Regiment of Private Prayer." In Foster and Smith, *Devotional Classics*, 87-93.

Camp, R. D., and Eric Hammel. *Lima-6: A Marine Company Commander in Vietnam*. New York: Pocket Books, 1989.

Caputo, Philip. *A Rumor of War*. New York: Henry Holt, 1977.

Carey, John, ed. *Eyewitness to History*. New York: Avon Books, 1987.

Carrier. TV. Directed by Maro Chermayeff. PBS. WETA, Icon Productions. 2008.

Carroll, Andrew, ed. *War Letters: Extraordinary Correspondence from American Wars*. New York: Scribner, 2001.

Cash, Carey. *A Table in the Presence: The Dramatic Account of How a U.S. Marine Battalion Experienced God's Presence Amidst the Chaos of the War in Iraq*. Nashville: W Publishing Group, 2004.

"Catechism of the Catholic Church." *Vatican.va*. http://www.vatican.va/archive/catechism/p123a12.htm (accessed 7 April 2008). 1033-1037.

Catholics United for the Faith. "Hell: The Self-Exclusion From God." *CUF.org*. http://www.cuf.org/faithfacts/details_view.asp?ffID=69 (accessed 7 April 2008).

Chamberlain, Joshua Lawrence. *The Passing of the Armies*. New York: Barnes and Noble, 2004.

Chambers, Larry. *Recondo: LRRPs in the 101st Airborne*. New York: Ballantine Books, 2003.

Chang, Jung. *Wild Swans: Three Daughters of China*. New York: Anchor Books, 1991.

Clark, Eugene Franklin. *The Secret of Inchon: The Untold Story of the Most Daring Covert Mission of the Korean War*. New York: G. P. Putnam's Sons, 2002.

Clark, Johnnie M. *Guns Up!* New York: Ballantine Books, 1984.

Clark, Mary T., ed. *An Aquinas Reader*. New York: Fordham University Press, 1972.

Clifton, Berry F., Jr. *Sky Soldiers: The Illustrated History of the Vietnam War*. New York: Bantam, 1987.

Coker, Jesse M. *My Unforgettable Memories of World War II*. Little Rock: Prestige Press, 2003.

Combat Film. VHS. Directed by Lawrence Ptkethly. South Burlington, VT: Annenberg/CPB Collection, 1994.

Combat Vietnam: To Hell and Beyond. DVD. Directed by 4th Infantry Division. BCI/Eclipse, 2000.

Constance, Harry, and Randall Fuerst. *Good to Go: The Life and Times of a Decorated Member of the U.S. Navy's Elite SEAL Team Two*. New York: Avon Books, 1997.

Coughlin, Jack, and Casey Kuhlman, with Donald A. Davis. *Shooter: The Autobiography of the Top-Ranked Marine Sniper*. New York: St. Martin's Paperbacks, 2005.

Crawford, George G., with James V. Lee. *When Surrender Was Not an Option*. Salado, TX: Salado Press, 2001.

Crisafulli, Chuck, and Kyra Thompson. *Go to Hell*. New York: Simon Spotlight Entertainment, 2005.

Crockett, William, ed. *Four Views on Hell*. Grand Rapids: Zondervan Publishing House, 1992.

Dallaire, Roméo. *Shake Hands with the Devil: The Failure of Humanity in Rwanda*. New York: Carroll and Graf Publishers, 2003.

Darby, William O., and William H. Baumer. *Darby's Rangers: We Led the Way*. New York: Presidio Press, 1980.

De Lecluse, Henri. *Comrades-In-Arms*. Edited by Roy Sandstrom. Translated by Jacques F. Dubois. Kent: The Kent State University Press, 1998.

De Wavrin, Jehan. "The Battle of Agincourt, 25 October 1415" in Carey, *Eyewitness to History*, 68-76.

Dear America: Letters Home from Vietnam. DVD. Directed by Bill Couturié. HBO Home Video, 2005.

Desert Storm: The Victory. VHS. Directed by Bernard Shaw. Universal City, CA: Turner Home Entertainment, 1991.

Desert Storm: The War Begins. VHS. Directed by Bernard Shaw. Universal City, CA:: Turner Home Entertainment, 1991.

Downfall. DVD. Directed by Oliver Hirschbiegel. Culver City, CA: Sony Home Entertainment, 2005

Draper, James David. "Antonio Gentili (c. 1519-1609): Altar Cross and Candlesticks." In *The Vatican Collections: The Papacy and Art*, edited by John O'Neill. New York: Harry N. Abrams, 1982.

Durant, Michael J. *In the Company of Heroes*. New York: New American Library, 2003.

Eliade, Mircea, ed. "Heaven and Hell" in *The Encyclopedia of Religion 6 [God - Ichi]*. New York: Macmillan Publishing Co., 1987.

Empey, Arthur Guy. *Over the Top*. New York: G. P. Putnam's Sons, 1917.

Engel, Richard. "Combat stress taking toll on U.S. soldiers." *MSNBC.com*, 2 November 2006. http://www.msnbc.msn.com/id/15433219/ (accessed 13 November 2006).

Exum, *This Man's Army: A Soldier's Story from the Front Lines of the War on Terrorism*. New York: Gotham Books, 2005.

Fick, Nathaniel. *One Bullet Away: The Making of a Marine Officer*. Boston: Houghton Mifflin Co., 2005.

Fiddes, Paul S. *The Creative Suffering of God*. Oxford: Clarendon Press, 1988.

Fisher, Sally. "Invention of the Cross" and "The Crucifixion" in *The Square Halo & Other Mysteries of Western Art: Images and Stories That Inspired Them*. New York: Harry N. Abrams, Inc., 1995.

Fleming, Daniel Johnson. *Christian Symbols in a World Community*. New York: Friendship Press, 1940.

Fletcher, William A. *Rebel Private, Front and Rear: Memoirs of a Confederate Soldier*. New York: Meridian, 1997.

Foster, Richard J. and James Bryan Smith, eds. *Devotional Classics: Selected Readings for Individuals and Groups*. San Francisco: HarperSanFrancisco, 1993.

Fremantle, Arthur J. L. *Three Months in the Southern States*. Lincoln: University of Nebraska Press, 1991.

Frothingham, O. B. "Religious Symbolism." *The New York Times*, 1 April 1883.

Full Metal Jacket. VHS. Directed by Stanley Kubrick. New York, NY: Warner Home Video, 1987.

Galantin, I. J. *Take Her Deep! A Submarine against Japan in World War II*. New York: Pocket Books, 1987.

Gantter, Raymond. *Roll Me Over: An Infantryman's World War II*. New York: Ivy Books, 1997.

Gingerich, Owen. *God's Universe*. Cambridge: Harvard University Press, 2006.

Glover, Jonathan. *Humanity: A Moral History of the Twentieth Century*. New Haven: Yale University Press, 1999.

Gordon, Ernest. *To End All Wars*. Grand Rapids: Zondervan, 2002.

Gorsuch, Geoff. *On Eagles' Wings: The Spiritual Odyssey of a Young American Pilot in Vietnam*. Colorado Springs: Navpress, 1989.

Grant, U. S. *Personal Memoirs of U. S. Grant*. New York: Da Capo, 1982.

Graves, Robert. *Good-bye to All That*. New York: Doubleday, 1989.

Gray, J. Glenn. *The Warriors: Reflections on Men in Battle*. Lincoln: University of Nebraska Press, 1998.

Green Berets,The. DVD. Directed by Ray Kellogg and John Wayne. New York, NY: Warner Home Video, 1997.

Grossman, Dave. *On Killing: The Psychological Cost of Learning to Kill in War and Society*. New York: Back Bay Books, 1996.

Hampton, Lynn. *The Fighting Strength: Memoirs of a Combat Nurse in Vietnam*. New York: Warner Books, 1990.

Hardwick, William H. *Down South: One Tour in Vietnam*. New York: Ballantine Books, 2004.

Hasker, William. *God, Time, and Knowledge*. Ithaca: Cornell University Press, 1989.

Hastings, Adrian, ed., "Hell" in *Oxford Companion to Christian Thought*. Oxford: Oxford University Press, 2000.

Haught, John. *God after Darwin: A Theology of Evolution*. Boulder: Westview Press, 2000.

Hearts and Minds. DVD. Directed by Peter Davis. Criterion Collection, 2002.

Herr, Michael. *Dispatches*. New York: Vintage International, 1977.

Herrington, Stuart A. *Stalking the Vietcong: Inside Operation Phoenix: A Personal Account.* New York: Ballantine Books, 1982.

Hillman, James. *A Terrible Love of War.* New York: Penguin Press, 2004.

Hodgins, Michael C. *Reluctant Warrior: A Marine's True Story of Duty and Heroism in Vietnam.* New York: Ivy Books, 1996.

Holley, Byron E. *Vietnam, 1968-1969: A Battalion Surgeon's Journal.* New York: Ivy Books, 1993.

Holmes, Arthur F., ed. *War and Christian Ethics: Classic Readings on the Morality of War.* Grand Rapids: Baker Book House, 1991.

Holmes, Richard. *Acts of War: The Behavior of Men in Battle.* New York: The Free Press, 1985.

Holton, Chuck. *A More Elite Soldier.* Sisters, OR: Multnomah Publishers, 2003.

Hontheim, Joseph. "Hell" in *The Catholic Encyclopedia* vol. 7. New York: Robert Appleton Company, 1910.

International Committee of the Red Cross. "The History of the Emblems." *ICRC.org.* http://www.icrc.org/web/eng/siteeng0.nsf/html/emblem-history (accessed 19 April 2008).

Jamieson Jr., Robert L. "Veteran gets rude welcome on Bainbridge." *Seattle-Post Intelligencer*, 9 July 2004.

Jeffrey, David Lyle ed., "Hell" and "Sheol" in *A Dictionary of Biblical Tradition in English Literature.* Grand Rapids: Eerdmans, 1992.

John Paul II. "Heaven, Hell and Purgatory." *EWTN.com.* Eternal Word Television Network. http://www.ewtn.com/library/PAPALDOC/JP2HEAVN.HTM (accessed 18 February 2008).

————. *Rise, Let Us Be on Our Way.* New York: Warner Books, 2004.

Johnson, James D. *Combat Chaplain: A Thirty-Year Vietnam Battle.* Denton, TX: University of North Texas Press, 2001.

Karkkainen, Veli-Matti. "'Evil, Love and the Left Hand of God': The Contribution of Luther's Theology of the Cross to an Evangelical Theology of Evil." *Evangelical Quarterly* 74, no. 3 (2002): 215-34.

Keefe, Derek. "There are Atheists in Foxholes." *Christianity Today*, 24 March 2008. http://blog.christianitytoday.com/ctliveblog/archives/2008/03/there_are_athei.html (accessed 28 March 2008).

Keegan, John. *A History of Warfare.* New York: Vintage Books, 1994.

Bibliography

———. *The Face of Battle*. New York: The Viking Press, 1976.

Kekes, John. *Facing Evil*. Princeton: Princeton University Press, 1990.

———. *Pluralism in Philosophy: Changing the Subject*. Ithaca: Cornell University Press, 2000.

Ketwig, John. *...and a Hard Rain Fell: A GI's True Story of the War in Vietnam*. Naperville, IL: Sourcebooks, 2002.

Kindsvatter, Peter S. *American Soldiers: Ground Combat in the World Wars, Korea, and Vietnam*. Lawrence: University of Kansas Press, 2003.

Klemperer, Victor. *I Will Bear Witness: A Diary of the Nazi Years*. Translated by Martin Chalmers. New York: The Modern Library, 2001.

Knappe, Siegfried, and Ted Brusaw. *Soldat: Reflections of a German Soldier, 1936-1949*. New York: Dell Publishing, 1992.

Kobo, Joseph. *Waiting in the Wing*. Vancouver: Nelson Word Ltd., 1994.

Labat, Gaston P. *Le Livre d'Or of the Canadian Contingents in South Africa*. Montreal, 1901.

Lanning, Michael Lee. *The Only War We Had: A Platoon Leader's Journal of Vietnam*. New York: Ivy Books, 1987.

Laubach, Frank. "Opening Windows to God." In Foster and Smith, *Devotional Classics*, 101-07.

Lawrence, T. E. *Revolt in the Desert*. New York: Tess Press, 2004.

Lawson, Ted W. *Thirty Seconds over Tokyo*. New York: Pocket Star Books, 2002.

Levi, Primo. *Survival in Auschwitz*. Translated by Stuart Woolf. New York: Collier Books, 1958.

Lewis, C. Day, ed. *The Collected Poems of Wilfred Owen*. New York: New Directions Book, 1963.

Lewis, C. S. *The Complete C. S. Lewis Signature Classics*. San Francisco: HarperSanFrancisco, 2002.

———. *The Joyful Christian*. New York: Collier Books, 1977.

Lewis, Jon E., ed. *War Diaries and Letters: Life on the Battlefield in the Words of the Ordinary Soldier*. New York: Carrol and Graf, 1999.

Lifton, Robert Jay. *Home from the War: Learning from Vietnam Veterans*. Boston: Beacon Press, 1992.

Lincoln, Abraham. Second Inaugural Address, 1865.

Linderer, Gary. *Six Silent Men: 101stLRP/Rangers* vol. III. New York: Ivy Books, 1997.

Linderman, Gerald F. *The World Within War*. Cambridge: Harvard University Press, 1997.

Linn, Brian AcAllister. *Guardians of Empire: The U.S. Army and the Pacific, 1902-1940*. Chapel Hill: The University of North Carolina Press, 1997.

Livingston, E.A., ed. "Constantine the Great," "Crucifix," "Crucifixion," "Exaltation of the Cross," "Gehenna," "Helena, St.," "Hell," "Prayer," and "Sheol" in *The Concise Oxford Dictionary of the Christian Church*. New York: Oxford University Press, 2006.

Lomax, Eric. *The Railway Man: A True Story of War, Remembrance, and Forgiveness*. New York: Ballantine Books, 1995.

Loyd, Anthony. *My War Gone By, I Miss It So*. New York: Penguin Books, 1999.

Luther, Martin. "Praying in Faith." In Foster and Smith, *Devotional Classics*, 115-120.

———. *Secular Authority: To What Extent It Should Be Obeyed*, 1523.

MacArthur, Douglas. *Reminiscences*. New York: Crest Books, 1964.

Mahedy, William P. *Out of the Night: The Spiritual Journey of Vietnam Vets*. New York: Ballantine Books, 1986.

Manchester, William. *Goodbye, Darkness: A Memoir of the Pacific War*. New York: Little, Brown and Company, 1980.

Mansfield, Stephen. *The Faith of the American Soldier*. Lake Mary, FL: Charisma House, 2005.

Marcinko, Richard, with John Weisman. *Rogue Warrior*. New York: Pocket Star Books, 1992.

Marius, Richard. *Martin Luther: The Christian between God and Death*. Cambridge: Belknap Press of Harvard University Press, 1999.

Martinez, Reynel. *Six Silent Men: 101st LRP/Rangers* vol. I. New York: Ballantine Books, 1997.

Marvicsin, Denis J., and Jerold A. Greenfield. *Maverick: The Personal War of a Vietnam Cobra Pilot*. New York: Jove Books, 1996.

Mason, Robert. *Chickenhawk: A Shattering Personal Account of the Helicopter War in Vietnam*. New York: Penguin, 1984.

Matsakis, Aphrodite. *Back From the Front: Combat Trauma, Love, and the Family*. Baltimore: Sidran Institute Press, 2007.

May, Felton and Bob Edgar. "In war, you can't count God to be on your side." *Arkansas Democrat Gazette* (October 1, 2006): 2J.

McCain, John. *Faith of My Fathers*. New York: Random House, 1999.

McDonald, Cherokee Paul. *Into the Green: A Reconnaissance by Fire*. New York: Plume Books, 2001.

McDonough, James R. *Platoon Leader: A Memoir of Command in Combat*. New York: Ballantine Publishing Group, 1985.

McManus, John C. *The Deadly Brotherhood: The American Combat Soldier in World War II*. New York: Ballantine Books, 1989.

Megellas, James. *All the Way to Berlin: A Paratrooper at War in Europe*. New York: Ballantine Books, 2003.

Merton, Thomas. "Ways of Meditation." In Foster and Smith, *Devotional Classics*, 65-72.

Middlebrook, Martin. *The First Day on the Somme, 1 July 1916*. New York: Penguin Books, 1971.

Miers, Earl Schenck, ed. *When the World Ended: The Diary of Emma LeConte*. Lincoln: University of Nebraska Press, 1987.

Miller, Jesse L. *Prisoner of Hope*. Englewood, CO: Cadence International, 1989.

Miller, Kenn. *Six Silent Men: 101st LRP/Rangers* vol. II. New York: Ballantine Books, 1997.

Miller, Kenneth. *Finding Darwin's God: A Scientist's Search for Common Ground between God and Evolution*. New York: HarperCollins, 1999.

Moore, Harold G. and Joseph L. Galloway. *We Were Soldiers Once...and Young*. New York: HarperTorch, 1992.

Moore, Robin. *The Hunt for bin Laden: Task Force Dagger*. New York: Ballantine Books, 2003.

Murphy, Audie. *To Hell and Back*. New York: Bantam Books, 1979.

Newby, Claude D. *It Took Heroes: A Cavalry Chaplain's Memoir of Vietnam*. New York: Ballantine Books, 2000.

"New Questions In Case Of Attack On Guardsman." *KIROTV.com*, 1 September 2006. http://www.kirotv.com/news/9765757/detail.html (accessed 2 December 2006).

Niebuhr, H. Richard. "War as Crucifixion" in *War in the Twentieth Century: Sources in Theological Ethics*, edited by Richard B. Miller. Louisville: Westminister/John Knox Press, 1992.

Niebuhr, Reinhold. *Beyond Tragedy: Essays on the Christian Interpretation of History*. New York: Charles Scribner's Sons, 1937.

———. "The Foolishness of the Cross and the Sense of History" in *Faith and History: A Comparison of Christian and Modern Views of History*. New York: Charles Scribner's Sons, 1949.

Noll, Mark. *America's God: From Jonathan Edwards to Abraham Lincoln*. Oxford: Oxford University Press, 2002.

Nolte, Claudia M. "A Theology of the Cross for South Africa." *Dialog: A Journal of Theology* 42, no. 1 (2003): 50-61.

North, Oliver, and David Roth. *One More Mission*. New York: HarperPaperbacks, 1993.

Norton, Bruce H. *Force Recon Diary, 1969*. New York: Ivy Books, 1991.

Nouwen, Henri J. M. "Bringing Solitude into Our Lives." In Foster and Smith, *Devotional Classics*, 80-86.

O'Brien, Thomas R. *Blessings from the Battlefield*. Huntington, IN: Our Sunday Visitor Publishing, 2002.

O'Brien, Tim. *If I Die in a Combat Zone, Box Me Up and Ship Me Home*. New York: Dell Publishing, 1973.

———. *The Things They Carried*. New York: Broadway Books, 1998.

O'Neill, James H. "The True Story of The Patton Prayer." *Patton HQ*. http://www.pattonhq.com/prayer.html (accessed 13 November 2006).

Onoda, Hiroo. *No Surrender: My Thirty-Year War*. Translated by Charles Terry. New York: Harper and Row Publishers, 1974.

Owen, Wilfred. *The Collected Poems of Wilfred Owen*. Edited by C. Day Lewis. New York: New Directions Books, 1963.

Palmer, Laura. *Shrapnel in the Heart: Letters and Remembrances from the Vietnam Veterans Memorial*. New York: Random House, 1987.

Parker Jr., James E. *Last Man Out: A Personal Account of the Vietnam War*. New York: Ballantine Books, 1996.

Parrish, John A. *12, 20 & 5: A Doctor's Year in Vietnam*. New York: Bantam Books, 1972.

Patton, George S., Jr., *War As I knew It*. New York: Bantam Books, 1975.

Paulson, Philip K. "I Was an Atheist in a Foxhole." *AmericanHumanist.org*. American Humanist Association. http://www.americanhumanist.org/humanism/fox hole.html (accessed 10 October 2006).

Peacocke, Arthur. *Paths from Science towards God: The End of All Our Exploring*. Oxford: Oneworld, 2001.

Perry, Marvin, ed. *Sources of the Western Tradition* vol. II. Boston: Houghton Mifflin Company, 2006.

Peterson, Robert A. "The Dark Side of Eternity: Hell as Eternal Conscious Punishment." *Christian Research Journal* 30, no. 4 (2007): 13-21.

Pfarrer, Chuck. *Warrior Soul: The Memoir of a Navy Seal*. New York: Ballantine Books, 2004.

Phillips, Rebecca. "Beliefwatch: Foxholes" *Newsweek* August 21/28, 2006, 18.

Pinnock, Clark. "The Destruction of the Finally Impenitent." *Criswell Theological Review* 4, Spr. (1990): 243-59.

──────, et al. *The Openness of God: A Biblical Challenge to the Traditional Understanding of God*. Downers Grove, IL: InterVarsity Press, 1994.

Platoon. DVD. Directed by Oliver Stone. MGM Home Entertainment, 2001.

Polkinghorne, John. *Faith of a Physicist*. Minneapolis: Fortress Press, 1996.

──────. *Faith, Science, and Understanding*. New Haven: Yale University Press, 2000.

──────. *One World: The Interaction of Science and Theology*. Princeton: Princeton University Press, 1986.

──────. *Science and Providence: God's Interaction with the World*. Boston: New Science Library, 1989.

Pollard, William G. *Chance and Providence: God's Action in a World Governed by Scientific Law*. New York: Charles Scribner's Sons, 1958.

Pyle, Ernie. *Here is Your War*. New York: Military Heritage Press, 1989.

Radike, Floyd W. *Across the Dark Islands: The War in the Pacific*. New York: Ballantine Books, 2003.

Rahner, Karl. *On the Theology of Death*. New York: Herder and Herder, 1961.

Ramsey, Bill. "There Are No Atheists in Foxholes." *SerraUS.org*. The USA Council of Serra International. http://www.serraus.org/serrausa/may03usa_a.htm (accessed 19 May 2008).

Remarque, Erich Maria. *All Quiet on the Western Front*. New York: Random House, 1982.

Return with Honor. DVD. Directed by Freida Lee Mock and Terry Sanders. Alexandria, VA: American Film Foundation, 1999.

Rhodes, Robert Hunt, ed. *All for the Union: The Civil War Diary and Letters of Elisha Hunt Rhodes*. New York: Orion Books, 1985.

Rickenbacker, Edward V. *Fighting the Flying Circus*. New York: Frederick A. Stokes Co., 1919.

Ricks, Thomas E. *Making the Corps*. New York: Simon and Schuster, 1997.

Risner, Robinson. *The Passing of the Night: My Seven Years as a Prisoner of the North Vietnamese*. New York: Ballantine Books, 1973.

Rosenblatt, Emil, and Ruth Rosenblatt, eds. *Hard Marching Every Day: The Civil War Letters of Private Wilbur Fisk, 1861-1865*. Lawrence: University Press of Kansas, 1983.

Rotundo, John L. and Don Ericson. *Charlie Rangers*. New York: Ivy Books, 1989.

Rowe, James N. *Five Years to Freedom: The True Story of a Vietnam POW*. New York: Ballantine Books, 1971.

Russell, Robert John et al., eds. "Describing God's Action" in *Chaos and Complexity: Scientific Perspectives on Divine Action* (Vatican City: Vatican Observatory Foundation, 2000.

Sack, John. *Company C: The Real War in Iraq*. New York: Avon Books, 1995.

Sajer, Guy. *The Forgotten Soldier*. Washington, D. C.: Potomac Books, Inc., 1971.

Sakai, Saburo, with Martin Caidin, and Fred Saito. *Samurai!* New York: Bantam Books, 1978.

Sanders, John. *The God Who Risks: A Theology of Providence*. Downers Grove, IL: InterVarsity Press, 1996.

Sassoon, Siegfried. *Memoirs of an Infantry Officer*. London: Faber and Faber, 1930.

Saving Private Ryan. DVD. Directed by Steven Spielberg. Burbank, CA: Dreamworks Home Entertainment, 1999.

Schaeffer, John, and Frank Schaeffer. *Keeping Faith: A Father-Son Story About Love and the United States Marine Corps*. New York: Carroll and Graf Publishers, 2002.

Schell, Jonathan. *The Real War: The Classic Reporting on the Vietnam War*. New York: Pantheon Books, 1987.

Schneider, Ches. *From Classrooms to Claymores: A Teacher at War in Vietnam*. New York: Ivy Books, 1999.

Schneider, Franz, and Charles Gullans, eds. and trans. *Last Letters from Stalingrad*. New York: The Hudson Review, Inc., 1961.

Schweitzer, Richard. *The Cross and the Trenches: Religious Faith and Doubt among British and American Great War Soldiers*. Westport, CT: Praeger, 2003.

Scott, Robert L. *God is My Co-Pilot*. New York: Charles Scribner's Sons, 1943.

Sherman, Ben. *Medic! The Story of a Conscientious Objector in the Vietnam War*. New York: Writer's Club Press, 2002.

Siemon-Netto, Uwe. *The Acquittal of God: A Theology for Vietnam Veterans*. New York: Pilgrim Press, 1990.

Sledge, E. B. *With the Old Breed: At Peleliu and Okinawa*. New York: Oxford University Press, 1981.

Smith, Constance I. "Descendit ad Inferos—Again," *Journal of the History of Ideas* 28, no. 1 (1967): 87-88.

Starinov, A. K. *Behind Fascist Lines: A Firsthand Account of Guerrilla Warfare During the Spanish Revolution*. New York: Ballantine Books, 2001.

Stavisky, Samuel E. *Marine Combat Correspondent: World War II in the Pacific*. New York: Ivy Books, 1999.

Stewart, Sidney. *Give Us This Day*. New York: Avon Books, 1990.

Stoffey, Bob. *Cleared Hot! The Diary of a Marine Combat Pilot in Vietnam*. New York: St. Martin's Paperbacks, 1992.

Stroup, Russell Cartwright. *Letters from the Pacific: A Combat Chaplain in World War II*. Edited by Richard Cartwright Austin. Columbia: University of Missouri Press, 2000.

Svan, Jennifer H. "Soldiers carry good luck along for rides into Iraq." *Stars and Stripes*, 12 October 2006. http://www.stripesonline.com/article.asp?section=104&article=39739&archive=true (accessed 13 November 2006).

Swinburne, Richard. *The Christian God.* Oxford: Clarendon Press, 1994.

Swofford, Anthony. *Jarhead: A Marine's Chronicle of the Gulf War and Other Battles.* New York: Pocket Books, 2003.

Ten Boom, Corrie. *A Prisoner and Yet ...* London: Christian Literature Crusade, 1954.

Terry, Wallace. *Bloods: An Oral History of the Vietnam War by Black Veterans.* New York: Ballantine Books, 1984.

Tertullian. *Treatises on Penance: on Penitence and on Purity.* Translated by William Saint. New York: Newman Press, 1959.

————. *The Ante-Nicene Fathers* vol. III. Edited by Alexander Roberts and James Donaldson. Grand Rapids: Wm. B. Eerdsman Publishing Company, 1980.

Thorne, Mister. "Atheists in Foxholes, Christians in Uniforms." *Humanist* 63, no. 3 (2003): 19-23.

To End All Wars. DVD. Directed by David L. Cunningham. Century City, CA: 20th Century Fox, 2001.

Toland, John. *Adolph Hitler* vol I. Garden City, NY: Doubleday & Co., 1976.

Toner, Patrick. "Limbo" in *The Catholic Encyclopedia* vol. 9. New York: Robert Appleton Company, 1910.

Tonsetic, Robert. *Warriors: An Infantryman's Memoir of Vietnam.* New York: Ballatine Books, 2004.

Tram, Dang Thuy. *Last Night I Dreamed of Peace: The Diary of Dang Thuy Tram.* Translated by Andrew X. Pham. New York: Harmony Books, 2007.

Tresidder, Jack, ed., "George, Saint," "Helena (Helen), Saint," "IHS," and "The True Cross" in *The Complete Dictionary of Symbols.* San Francisco: Chronicle Books, 2005.

Turnipseed, Joel. *Baghdad Express: A Gulf War Memoir.* New York: Penguin Books, 2003.

Underhill, Evelyn. "What Do We Mean by Prayer?" In Foster and Smith, *Devotional Classics*, 94-100.

Van Scott, Miriam. "Augustine, Saint," "Christian Hell," and "City of God" in *Encyclopedia of Hell.* New York: St. Martin's Press, 1998.

Van Zanten, William. *Don't Bunch Up: One Marine's Story.* New York: Ballantine Books, 1993.

Vaughan, Edwin Campion. *Some Desperate Glory: The World War I Diary of a British Officer, 1917.* New York: Henry Holt and Company, 1981.

Vietnam: A Television History. VHS. Directed by Matthew Collins and Rocky Collins. WGBH Boston and Central Independent Television/UK, 1993.

Ward, Joseph T. *Dear Mom: A Sniper's Vietnam.* New York: Ivy Books, 1991.

Warr, Nicholas. *Phase Line Green: The Battle for Hue, 1968.* New York: Ivy Books, 1997.

Watkins, Sam. *Co Aytch: A Confederate Memoir of the Civil War.* New York: Touchstone, 2003.

Watson, C. Hoyt. *The Amazing Story of Sergeant Jacob DeShazer.* Winona Lake, IN: Light and Life Press, 1950.

Waugh, Billy, with Tim Keown. *Hunting the Jackal: A Special Forces and CIA Soldier's Fifty Years on the Frontlines of the War Against Terrorism.* New York: Avon-Books, 2004.

We Were Soldiers. DVD. Directed by Randall Wallace. Paramount Home Entertainment, 2002.

Wellum, Geoffrey. *First Light.* New York: Penguin Books, 2002.

Whitman, Walt. *Memoranda during the War.* Edited by Pete Coviello. New York: Oxford University Press, 1990.

Wiesel, Elie. *Night.* New York: Bantam Books, 1960.

————. *All Rivers Run to the Sea: Memoirs.* New York: Schocken Books, 1995.

Williams, Buzz. *Spare Parts: A Marine Reservist's Journey from Campus to Combat in 38 Days.* New York: Gotham Books, 2004.

Wilson, George. *If You Survive.* New York: Ballantine Books, 1987.

Winter Soldier. DVD. Directed by Winterfilm Collective. New Yorker Video, 1972.

Witkop, Philipp, ed. *German Students' War Letters.* Philadelphia: Pine Street Books, 2002.

Wright, Evan. *Generation Kill: Devil Dogs, Iceman, Captain America, and the New Face of American War.* New York: G. P. Putnam's Sons, 2004.

Wright, J. Robert, ed. *Readings for the Daily Office from the Early Church.* New York: Church Publishing Incorporated, 1991.

Zinsmeister, Karl. *Boots on the Ground: A Month with the 82nd Airborne in the Battle for Iraq.* New York: St. Martin's Press, 2003.